Spies Don't Cry

A Screenplay

Kenneth Frawley

Food for thought:

Does one ever really know about one's origins?

Is the past, the past, or is it everlasting, something one can never be free of?

Is there really no such thing as happily ever after?

Spies Don't Cry

by Kenneth Frawley

From Bonkers Publishing

Photographs by Pexels

Dedications

A list of great writers, professors and mentors I admire and owe a huge debt to would truly run pages. So, I shall simply offer to all of them my sincerest, and heartfelt gratitude. However, I must single out Ms Linda Palmer, a brilliant instructor I studied with at UCLA. I cannot begin to explain how influential she has been. Now, although it may have been merely a motivational technique of hers to leave a voice message praising a class submission of mine, yet no other professor took the time to ring and say:

"Ken, it's brilliant! Very, very clever! I'm so very proud of you. I know a producer who would really like your piece. Let's discuss getting it to him in class. Very nice!"

Inspirational ploy or not, my thanks to Ms Palmer and all my dedicated professors for their instruction and support, nonetheless. I greatly admire them all. Indeed, I am humbled, and consider myself very fortunate to have studied under them. Truly!

Spies Don't Cry

by

Kenneth F. Frawley

FADE IN:

EXT. ALGERIAN DESERT - NIGHT

Brilliant moonlight is an obstacle as EVAN RHODES, tall,
exceptionally fit man of 60, clad in black military-
style coveralls, sneaks through a field of concrete
huts. Reaching one, he peers into a cellar-like window.

INT. LABORATORY - NIGHT - RHODES' POV

The vast, stark underground laboratory is a sea of
tables, each loaded with culture-filled petri dishes,
tended to by workers clad in protective HAZMAT suits.

EXT. ALGERIAN DESERT - NIGHT

Rhodes sets and mounts a small, timed C4 charge onto the
structure, then quickly moves on to another. There,
through a similarly small window, Rhodes is horrified by
what he discovers.

INT. INFIRMARY - NIGHT - RHODES' POV

The sterile room is filled with the dead and horribly
ill strapped to cots. The living convulse and vomit,
their faces covered with red blotches and bleeding
lesions, contort with pain.

                    RHODES (O.S.)
              Christ almighty!

EXT. ALGERIAN DESERT - NIGHT

In the distance an armed, SOLDIER is alarmed when his
large GERMAN SHEPHERD becomes agitated. He unleashes it.

Rounding the corner, the dog races. Rhodes hurries to
set another C4 charge, but fumbles in haste. Finally,
the device responds. Rhodes grabs his satchel and runs
for the cut-away in the wire fencing.

Winded, Rhodes stops. The dog salivates at the sight of
him. As it springs, Rhodes swings his bag at the dog's
head. It's out.

                    RHODES
              Sorry, ol' man. I'm afraid I'm
              too old for the hundred meters.

Alerted by the dog's whimper, SOLDIER readies his rifle
and rushes toward it.

Rhodes dives through the cut-away, rolls flat on the
ground, produces a silenced handgun, leans on elbows,
takes aim, then coolly, shoots the arriving SOLDIER.

Rhodes jumps down on to the road below, takes a deep
breath, sheds the coveralls, revealing a well-tailored
Italian suit.

Now collected, Rhodes pulls out a cigar and saunters
over to the lone, war-torn nightclub, CLUB FELICITE,
just up the empty, very third-world street.

INT. CLUB FELICITE - NIGHT

The symbol of sophistication and style, Rhodes looks out
of place as he casually pauses to check his watch and
light his cigar in the seedy dive.

With a worn dance floor serving as a stage, a cheap and
slightly overweight belly dancer puts on a frighteningly
tasteless floorshow.

EXT. BUNKER FIELD - NIGHT

All quiet and calm. BOOM! Suddenly, the field is alight.

INT. CLUB FELICITE - NIGHT

Rocked by the commotion, the crowd panics, scurries out.
Rhodes, ridiculously calm, walks to the bar, where PABLO,
dapper, 60, sits, calmly staring into his drink.

A large, brutish BARTENDER has remained.

                    RHODES
          Gimlet, s'il vous plait.

Fierce hatred in his eye, the oaf tends to the request.

                    PABLO
               (Spanish accent)
          We have to stop meeting like this.

                    RHODES
          Don't tell me thirty years of
                    (MORE)

                    RHODES (cont.)
battling psychopaths and lounging
in such fine settings as this is
enough for you?

                    PABLO
Perhaps.

                    RHODES
Well, I should think we've
put an end to T.E.S.'s
chemical weapons threat tonight.

                    PABLO
I am afraid our efforts here may
only supply Rhumandi with reason
for retaliation.

With a look of distain, BARTENDER sets Rhodes' drink
down hard on the bar. Cheekily, Rhodes acknowledges him
with an all-too grateful smile and a nod.

                    RHODES
                  (to Pablo)
Since when has our old friend
ever needed a reason to inflict
pain and suffering?

                    PABLO
Nevertheless, you had better be--
                    RHODES
--on the next boat to Marseilles?
                  (puts drink on bar)
Seems a shame to leave such a
lovely place.

In his glass, Rhodes catches reflection of a large grimy
MAN about to strike him from behind. He grabs his drink,
spins round quickly, tossing the liquid into the man's
face. Follows with the glass to the head.
Stunned, the man drops to one knee. Rhodes quickly
finishes him off with a barstool over the head.

Turning to Pablo, Rhodes finds BARTENDER removing a
knife from Pablo's back, whilst focusing on Rhodes.

                    RHODES (cont.)
I'm too old for this. Sure you
wouldn't rather call it a draw?

The oaf simply snarls back.

> RHODES (cont.)
> I thought not.
> (points to glass on floor)
> Mind the glass.

The ploy works. BARTENDER flinches, Rhodes scores with a stiff right. A fight for the knife ensues. BARTENDER is too young, too large, too strong. He easily takes hold of Rhodes and slowly raises the blade.

Rhodes uses his feet to shove off against a wall, sends them back onto a barstool and into the bar. Then, without hesitation, Rhodes sinks the huge blade through the man's thigh and into the barstool.

As the behemoth bellows out in agony, Rhodes quickly grabs a bottle from the bar and knocks him cold. He then straightens himself, and taps Pablo's shoulder.

> RHODES (cont.)
> I shall miss you, my old friend.

Making for the door, Rhodes notices the belly dancer, frozen with shock. He gently applauds her.

> RHODES (cont.)
> Riveting. Simply riveting.

He then saunters out the back door.

EXT. ALGERIAN STREET - NIGHT

The mayhem inside continues outdoors. As Rhodes strolls out of the club and into the night, he spots many of the panic-stricken patrons diving onto an old truck.

Spotting running SOLDIERS, he reluctantly sprints for the truck. But, as it pulls away, Rhodes is unable to catch it. Winded, he hunches to catch his breath.

Out of nowhere, a voice commands attention.

> KAZALI'S VOICE (O.S.)
> I'm afraid you shall miss your
> boat, Monsieur Rhodes.

Rhodes turns to behold the dark, very Mediterranean looking CAPTAIN KAZALI, 55, with an ego larger than his physical stature, accompanied by several SOLDIERS.

> RHODES
> How fortunate. Now I can catch
> the second show.

> KAZALI
> I should not count on that.

> RHODES
> Really? Pity.

> KAZALI
> The entertainment is that good, no?

> RHODES
> They're pinned to their seats.

Kazali gestures and soldiers take Rhodes into custody.

EXT. WELSH COUNTRY COTTAGE - DAY

The lush green, rural setting is stunning. The cottage and the day are picture perfect. NELLY, lovely, middle-aged Cinderella, is visible through the window.

Suddenly, the portrait is spoilt by the appearance of a BLACK MERCEDES saloon creeping to a stop. Two bookish men in brown tweed, bow ties, and glasses emerge.

MR. HANDKERCHIEF, whose blazer sports elbow patches, carries a handkerchief. While MR. HANDYCAM shoots video from the hip as they sneakily approach the house.

Reaching the cottage unobserved, they eye their prey through the unlocked front door and slither in.

INT. NELLY'S KITCHEN - DAY

At the sink, water running, Nelly doesn't hear the intruders before they are upon her.

Handkerchief quickly rams his handkerchief into her mouth. Handycam manages to hand him a pair of handcuffs whilst videotaping.

Hands cuffed behind her, she's led into the sitting room.

En route, they bump the dining table, knocking over the floral bouquet and birthday card. Water from the vase smears the inscription: "HAPPY BIRTHDAY, MUM!"

INT. SITTING ROOM - DAY

Handkerchief sits Nelly on the sofa, then moves behind her. Handycam, still recording, takes a seat facing her as Handkerchief hurries a plastic bag over her head. Nelly struggles violently as Handkerchief firmly holds her down by neck and shoulders. Handycam records all.

INT. UNIVERSITY LECTURE HALL - DAY

EVAN TYDFIL, 32, tall, handsome, casually stylish, lectures to a large group of students. The class, particularly the female assemblage, is captivated.

> EVAN
> Actually, the sophists were not, technically speaking, philosophers. They were simply a group of learned opportunists who taught any subject for which there was popular demand--
> (notices wall clock)
> Unfortunately, we'll have to save this for next time. --Remember, papers are due next week.

He stuffs papers into a satchel, slings it over a shoulder and makes his way out through a group of attentive girls.

INT. CORRIDOR - DAY

Entering the corridor, Evan is met by HOLLING, 45, disheveled and very stressed.

> HOLLING
> I'm glad I caught you.

> EVAN
> I thought I'd taught you to iron.

> HOLLING
> I know I'm a bit of a nuisance, but I desperately need your help.

EVAN
(eyeing Holling's clothes)
So I gather.

HOLLING
Look, as the youngest chair
this institution has ever--

EVAN
Institution? Chair? No!
Whatever it is, no! How many
times must I tell you? I'm
only interested in--

HOLLING
The quiet life. Yes, I know--

EVAN
I simply will not be roped
into anything--

HOLLING
Political. Yes, I know. But--

EVAN
Global, national or university,
I want none to do with politics.

HOLLING
I'm not asking you to join the
fundraising committee, nothing
so despicable. I was simply
hoping you could help me pen a
few words of gratitude to our
benefactors. You know how bad
I am at this sort of thing.

EVAN
Sorry. Off to Nelly's. It's
her birthday.

HOLLING
Tomorrow, then?

EVAN
I've got essay and exams to--

HOLLING
How long can that take Mr. Brilliant?

EVAN
You don't need any help. You're a
master in the art of groveling.

He bolts off through a door and out of the building.

EXT. CAMPUS/ABERYSTWYTH, WALES - DAY

SAMANTHA, 22, very pretty, waits by a rack of bicycles.
Her face lights up when Evan emerges from the building.

SAMANTHA
Hello, Evan.

EVAN
I prefer Professor Tydfil.

SAMANTHA
But Evan is so much sweeter.
Don't you think?

EVAN
I really haven't given it
much thought.

SAMANTHA
Have you given any thought to
letting me cook dinner for you
some evening?

He unlocks one of the bicycles.

EVAN
We've had this discussion be--

SAMANTHA
It doesn't have to be dinner.
Maybe we could just pop down
the pub? I'm free right now--

He hops onto his mountain bike without offering a reply.

SAMANTHA (cont.)
Just a quick one, then?

EVAN
I'm a professor at this
university. It wouldn't do for
me to be dating the student body.

                    SAMANTHA
     Not the student body, just this one.

                    EVAN
     Samantha--

                    SAMANTHA
     Wasn't it Epicurus who said we
     should seek to rid ourselves of
     our desires by satisfying them
     completely?

                    EVAN
     He also said we need to look
     ahead to the consequences of
     all the pleasures we enjoy.

Without a comeback, her face reveals a bitter defeat.

                    EVAN (cont.)
     Look, any other time I'd love to.
     Really. But right now I've just
     got too much-- You understand,
     don't you?

Reluctantly, she nods.

                    EVAN (cont.)
     You're very, very sweet. Now,
     I'll see that lovely face in
     class. With essay in hand, right?

With that he peddles off, through the campus.

EXT. ABERYSTWYTH STREET - DAY

Gliding through the street, Evan spots the parked BLACK
MERCEDES and MR. Bale, 60, working in his garden.

                    MR. BALE
     Wish Nelly a very happy birthday
     for me, Professor?

                    EVAN
     Will do. She'll be very pleased
     you remembered.

                    MR. BALE
     She's a good woman, your mum.

Out of nowhere, the BLACK MERCEDES comes to a screeching halt in front of Evan, knocking him to the ground. As the two men jump out, Mr. Bale races into his cottage.

As Handkerchief, with gun drawn, moves in for a point-blank execution, Handycam is again ready with camera.

> EVAN
> What the bloody--!

Out of the corner of his eye, Evan spots the danger, but keeps his focus on his satchel as he gets to his feet.

> EVAN (cont.)
> Please forgive me. It's my
> fault. I didn't see you there--

Just as Handkerchief moves within range, Evan knocks the gun from his hand with the satchel, then quickly follows with a second swing to the man's head.

With Handkerchief unconscious, Evan and Handycam lock eyes. Coolly, Handycam tosses his camera into the car, removes his spectacles and confidently approaches.

He fakes a punch. Evan swings the pack. Handycam dodges it, grabs it and swings Evan against the MERCEDES. He then chucks the pack and slips a hand into his coat.

Evan quickly charges bull-like. Handycam dodges again. Evan's stumble brings a smile to Handycam's face and he readies himself to finish the job by hand.

They square off.

Quickly, Handycam is hit by a left jab, then another, and another. Unable to avoid them, he rages, only to be put down with by Evan's strong right hang.

As Mr. Bale arrives, Evan retrieves the handgun from Handycam's pocket, and Handkerchief's from the ground.

> EVAN
> (to villains)
> I've three words for you,
> anger management therapy.

                    MR. BALE
                    (to Evan)
        I rang the police. --I reckoned
        they'd need someone to rescue them.

                    MR. BALE
                    (to villains)
        You lads aren't from around here,
        are you? The professor's boxing
        prowess is legend in these parts.

The two attackers stagger to their car and race off.
Evan hands Mr. Bale the guns, then climbs onto his bike.

                    MR. BALE
        What on earth was that all about?

                    EVAN
        No idea. Road rage, perhaps?

Evan rides off.

EXT. NELLY'S COTTAGE - DAY

Approaching the front door, Evan notices it's ajar.

INT. NELLY'S LIVING ROOM - DAY

Calling out, Evan enters, he spots Nelly slumped on the
sofa. He rushes to her and rips the bag from her head.

Too late, he lets loose the yowl of a wounded wolf.

EXT. NELLY'S COTTAGE - NIGHT

Parked police cars identify a crime scene. A sleek BMW
rolls to a stop in front of the cottage. HAWKINS and
WILLIAMS, both 45, very well clad, emerge from the car
and approach the house.

INT. NELLY'S LIVING ROOM - NIGHT

Evan sits in utter disbelief, as police examine the
scene. CONNELL, 50, the local inspector, attempts to
distract Evan as Nelly's bagged body is carried out.

                    CONNELL
        Can I get you anything? A drink?

Nothing.

                    CONNELL (cont.)
          Let me have one of the lads stay
          with you tonight, all right?

Again, nothing. Simultaneously, Hawkins and Williams
enter the house. Connell recognizes them, and they him.

                    CONNELL (cont.)
          What does MI6 want with this?

                    WILLIAMS
          We'd like a word with Mr. Tydfil.

                    CONNELL
          This is not a good time.

                    HAWKINS
          Mr. Tydfil. Alone!

Hesitantly, Connell shepherds his men out.

                    EVAN
          Oi! There's been a murder--

                    HAWKINS
          We are very sorry for your loss.

                    WILLIAMS
                    (to Evan)
          We are informed that there was
          an attack on your life today,
          as well. Is this correct, sir?

                    HAWKINS
          Two men? A black Merc?

Surprise paints Evan's face.

                    HAWKINS (cont.)
          You'll have to come with us, sir.

                    EVAN
          What for?

                    HAWKINS
          You'll be fully briefed on the
          matter when we get to London.

                    EVAN
London? Are you mad? I'm not
going anywhere! My mum has--

                  HAWKINS
And I'll need your phone, sir.

                    EVAN
What?

                  HAWKINS
They are tracking your phone.

                    EVAN
They?

Hawkins extends one hand. Reluctantly, Evan hand over
his phone, only to watch Hawkins toss it onto the sofa.

                  HAWKINS
              (gesturing to door)
After you, sir.

INT. MANNINGTON'S OFFICE - NIGHT

The stately, wood paneled, traditional room is
impressive. Evan, alone, is too anxious to notice.

MANNINGTON, distinguished, impeccably dressed, tall, 60,
charges in. JAMMISSON, equally well dressed, 60, follows.

                  MANNINGTON
I cannot tell you how-- I
promise, there will be hell--

                    EVAN
You knew my mother?

                  MANNINGTON
For many years, yes. However,
I regret, the circumstances of
our acquaintance afforded me
the pleasure of meeting with
her on only a few occasions.

                    EVAN
Circumstances? Acquaintance?

Mannington steps over to a large carafe.

MANNINGTON
Sherry? --No, wait, I seem to
recall you're a Bordeaux man--

EVAN
Sod the drink! Just what the
bloody hell is going on here?
And how on earth would you know
what I prefer to drink?

MANINGTON
Forgive me, please. This is Jammisson,
my confidential executive assistant.

JAMMISSON
(to Evan)
Very pleased to meet you, Mr. Rho--,
Mr. Tydfil, my sincerest condolences.

Evan notices Jammisson's verbal stumble.

MANINGTON
I'm Nigel Mannington, Section Chief,
Commander in Charge, MI6 International—
Well, let's skip all that for now.
...We've never met. No, correct that.
We met once, when you were three
years old. I knew your mother some
35 years. Yes, even before you--

EVAN
I never heard--

MANNINGTON
Of course not. It's that secrecy
that has kept both of you alive.

EVAN
And now?

MANNINGTON
I fear there may be a leak--

EVAN
Ring for a plumber, then.

MANNINGTON
(to Jammisson)
Two scotches, please.

15

>   JAMMISSON
>   Yes, sir.

He strides out dutifully.

>   EVAN
>   Are you sure you're talking about
>   the right person, Nelly Tydfil?

>   MANNINGTON
>   You are Evan Tydfil. Born 32
>   years ago in Nice, France to
>   Nelly Tydfil, 23, a fashion
>   model living on the Cote d'Azur—
>   After your birth she took you
>   to Swansea, where the two of
>   you lived with her parents.

Jammisson returns with tray carrying glasses and bottle.

>   MANNINGTON (cont.)
>   (to Jammisson)
>   Ah, thank you.
>   (to Evan)
>   You attended university at Cardiff
>   and, later, at the Sorbonne.

Jammisson opens, pours delivers two pours.

>   MANNINGTON (cont.)
>   (to Evan)
>   Currently, you teach Philosophy,
>   French, Boxing and Fencing at the
>   University of Aberystwyth.
>   (to Jammisson)
>   Quite a chip off the ol' block, eh?

>   JAMMISSON
>   Indeed, sir.

>   EVAN
>   Why should any of that interest
>   MI6? Are you trying to tell me
>   my mother was a spy, or something?

Mannington takes in a deep breath.

                    MANNINGTON
For 35 years now, I have had the
great pleasure of working with the
single most accomplished MI6
operative that has ever been part
of this organisation. His name is
Evan Rhodes. And he, I must now
tell you, is your father.

                    EVAN
Look, I don't know what kind of
sick game this is, but my
father's name--

                    MANNINGTON
Neil. Stephen Neil. He was a
commander in the Royal Navy and
was killed by a terrorist missile
just off the coast of Beirut.

                    EVAN
If you know all that, then what's--

                    MANNINGTON
All that is true about Mr. Neil,
except he is not your father.
He's only a name we had put on
the birth record. A name selected
because he was the right age, he
had no family to complicate matters,
and, most importantly, he was dead.

Evan slumps back into his chair.

                    MANNINGTON (cont.)
My good friend Rhodes and your mother,
were very much that rare, perfectly
happy couple. Normally, they would
have built a life together. Except
for one thing, your father is a
British agent.

                    EVAN
Is?

                    MANNINGTON
Is one of ours, a distinction
that, unfortunately, also comes
                    (MORE)

> MANNINGTON (cont.)
> with a great number of dangerous
> adversaries. When you came along,
> your parents realised there was
> something more important than
> their life together. --Believe me,
> it wasn't an easy decision for them.

He gestures to Jammisson for more Scotch.

> MANNINGTON (cont.)
> I thought it best you take your
> mother's surname name. I promised
> to keep watch over the two of you,
> send money and report-- He is
> very proud, you know.

> EVAN
> Wait! You actually expect me to--

> JAMMISSON
> to Mannington)
> It is time, sir.

> MANNINGTON
> Thank you, Jammisson.
> (to Evan)
> Quickly, we must go.

> EVAN
> Go? Where to?

Mannington and Jammisson hurry Evan out.

INT. CORRIDOR - NIGHT

In the long, narrow corridor, several AGENTS, including
Hawkins and Williams, spring to life as Mannington,
Jammisson and Evan appear.

> MANNINGTON
> Hawkins and his team will take
> you to a safe place.

The agents hover around Evan as the group proceeds.

> EVAN (cont.)
> Are you sure all this isn't the
> result of some computer error or--

> MANNINGTON
> Rhodes is no computer error. He's
> a British operative. The best
> there has--

> EVAN
> Are you seriously trying to tell me
> my father is James Bond or someth--

Mannington abruptly halts the procession.

> MANNINGTON
> I beg your pardon! Bond is a mere
> comic strip. What we are talking
> about here is a very real person.
> A man who has the respect and
> admiration of every single one of
> the faces you see before you. A
> man who set the standards these
> operatives now employ.

> EVAN
> So why Nelly, then? What the hell
> has she got to do with any of this?

> MANNINGTON
> Her love, your father, my friend,
>   (gestures at agents)
> their mentor, has been taken
> prisoner by an extremely ruthless
> terrorist group-- A group, which
> has also decided, it wants the heads
> of everyone in his little family.
> --Now, if you will, this way please.

The procession resumes its pace. Quickly reaching the
corridor end, it blasts through the large metal doors.

INT. UNDERGROUND CAR PARK - NIGHT

Evan, led by Mannington, Jammisson and their entourage,
burst in. An elegant BMW saloon awaits. More AGENTS
secure the area. Hawkins and Williams are among them.

> EVAN
>   (to Mannington)
> Look, this is all very impressive,
> but you can't seriously expect me
>   (MORE)

EVAN (cont.)
to go into hiding just now. I've
a funeral to arrange, exams to
prepare. I must get back as--

MANNINGTON
I'm afraid that's impossible.

EVAN
Sorry?

MANNINGTON
Maybe one day you can return.

EVAN
What?

MANNINGTON
I have given my word. And these
villains are professionals!

EVAN
Now hang on! You just can't make
promises that involve my life,
ones that I have never agreed to.

Mannington signals Hawkins to usher Evan into the car.

MANNINGTON
As I explained, I've always done.

EVAN (cont.)
And what about this Rhodes?

MANNINGTON
Must dash. Hawkins and Williams
will brief you-- Safe journey.

INT. CAR - MORNING

TWO AGENTS climb into the front. Hawkins and Williams
remain in the back with Evan as they accelerate away.

EVAN
Well, get on with it, then.

Hawkins, cold as a Greenland winter, speaks with a black
and white precision.

                    HAWKINS
        Rhodes took out what we suspected
        to be a chemical weapons site TES
        had in Algeria.

                    WILLIAMS
        And now all bloody hell has
        broken lose.

                    HAWKINS
        Number 10 and Washington, have
        just ten days to come up with
        two trillion in US dollars. If
        not, TES promises to unleash an
        unholy nightmare upon a major
        city in America or Europe.

                    EVAN
        Who's Tess?

                    WILLIAMS
        Terrorism, Execution and Sacrifice.

                    EVAN
        What kind of nightmare?

                    HAWKINS
        The worst.

                    WILLIAMS
        An explosive device containing
        a great quantity of a hazardous
        compound.

                    HAWKINS
        We suspect zinc cadmium sulfide.

                    WILLIAMS
        A compound they've had some
        considerable success with in--

                    EVAN
        Success? Jesus!

                    WILLIAMS
        Enough so that the leaders of
        the free world are considering payment.

                    HAWKINS
Supposedly.

                    EVAN
And if they don't?

                    HAWKINS
We don't fund terrorists.

                    EVAN
And what about Rhodes?

                    WILLIAMS
A broadcasted execution, once--

                    EVAN
Once what?

                    HAWKINS
Your corpse is shown to Rhodes.

                    WILLIAMS
Which is why you must follow our
instructions to the letter.

                    EVAN
That's it? Hide me to buy time?
Then get Rhodes?

                    WILLIAMS
The device is the priority.

                    EVAN
Hang on! After all you say he's
done for the nation, you're not--

                    HAWKINS
There's no such thing as happily
ever after, especially for a
British agent.

                    WILLIAMS
It's procedure. Rhodes would
expect nothing else.

                    HAWKINS
That boxing lesson you gave
Rhumandi's men bought your
father some time.

                    WILLIAMS
It may have bought us all some.

                    HAWKINS
You stay alive, Rhodes stays alive.

                    EVAN
Rhumandi?

                    HAWKINS
The leader of TES.

                    WILLIAMS
Ever hear of things like Gulf
War Syndrome? ...That's TES.

Due to STREET WORKERS, traffic bottlenecks. Evan sees
TWO MIDDLE-EASTERN MEN approaching the car. He tenses.
The others seem unconcerned as the two men pass the car
without incident. Evan sighs relief.

                    WILLIAMS (cont.)
Rhumandi's yacht has been located
in Athens harbour. So, with a
little luck--

                    HAWKINS
                    (to Evan)
Do what we tell you and you and
your father just might live--

Suddenly, the BLACK MERCEDES comes to a screeching halt
before them. Handycam and Handkerchief blast out firing.

Adrenaline fills the MI6 car.

                    HAWKINS
Get down!

Suddenly TWO STREET WORKERS join in on the assault. The
barrage is overwhelming. MI6 agents can barely return
fire. The two agents in front of the car die quickly.
Bullets rip through Williams' window and head. Hawkins
opens the door, using it as shielding as he fires. He
grabs Williams' gun, hands it to Evan.

                    HAWKINS
                    (waves Evan out)
Go!

As Evan dashes out, Hawkins is riddled with bullets.

EXT. LONDON STREET - DAY

Dashing under a lorry parked nearby, Evan loses his grip
on the handgun. It slides to a stop ten feet away.

Yet, as the assassins reach the BMW to survey their
work, Evan has no time to retrieve it and scurries under
the lorry to the pavement without it.

Not finding Evan, Handkerchief screams out frustration.
Handycam spots Evan running and opens fire, shooting
recklessly through the volume of pedestrians and cars.

Handkerchief waves on one STREET WORKER after Evan.

EXT. ANOTHER LONDON STREET - DAY

Rounding a corner, Evan quickly positions himself
against a building to take his pursuer by surprise.

An ELDERLY GENT, with umbrella as walking stick, is in
harm's way. Evan quickly steers him against the wall and
takes the startled man's umbrella.

                    EVAN
          Pardon me a moment, sir.

Using the umbrella with Katana sword-like mastery, Evan
puts down the STREET WORKER, then returns the umbrella.

                    EVAN (cont.)
               (to Elderly Gent)
          Just the thing for battling the
          storm. Many thanks!

EXT. LONDON STREET - DAY

Sirens fill the air. Handycam angrily pounds the roof of
the car before he, and Handkerchief, race off.

EXT. ANOTHER LONDON STREET - DAY

Evan strides another block, spots THE CLARENCE, a corner
pub, checks over his shoulder, then rushes inside.

INT. THE CLARENCE PUB - DAY

It's empty. The LANDLORD and WIFE, both 55, are setting up shop. Evan charges in.

Evan looks about the whole of the pub.

> LANDLORD
> What can I get you, sir?

> EVAN
> I need a phone!

Noticing the stress in Evan's face, the Landlord retrieves a mobile from his pocket and hands it to Evan.

> LANDLORD
> I'll fetch you a cupper.

Evan dials hurriedly.

WOMAN'S VOICE is on the other end.

> WOMAN (O.S)
> What's your emergency?

> EVAN (cont.)
> (into phone)
> Get a hold of Mannington at MI6--
> Mannington! MI6! Got it? --Yes,
> you can. I don't know the number.
> It's life and death. Have him
> ring Evan at this number-- Now!

He rings off, just as tea arrives.

> LANDLORD
> Reckoned you could do with a
> couple scones to go with your
> tea. They're the wife's.

> EVAN
> Thanks. They look--

The phone rings. Evan dives for it.

> EVAN
> Mannington?

MANNINGTON'S VOICE is on the other end.

                    MANNINGTON (O.S)
        Evan?

                    EVAN
        They're dead! Hawkins, Williams,
        the others-- They're all dead.

INT. MANNINGTON'S OFFICE - SAME TIME

                    MANNINGTON
        Stay there. A car's on the way.

INTERCUT - PHONE CONVERSATION

                    EVAN
        What? How? You don't know where--

                    MANNINGTON
        GPS from the phone you're using.

                    EVAN
        Bloody hell!

                    MANNINGTON
        Look, just relax! We're on the--

                    EVAN
        But they're on to you, sir?

                    MANNINGTON
        Try to remain calm.

                    EVAN
        Ah, right! Silly me! Why not
        simply switch into chill mode?

                    MANNINGTON
        Just relax, we're on the way.

                    EVAN
        Perhaps I should stay on the move.

                    MANNINGTON
        No! Absolutely not! Remain where--

                    EVAN
        But, sir--

                    MANNINGTON
          Look, I understand your reaction.
          You've been through a terrible--

                    EVAN
          I'm glad you understand, because I
          don't understand a bloody thing!
          Yesterday my mother was alive and
          well. Yesterday I had a home, a
          career. Today I'm on the endangered
          species list!

                    MANNINGTON
          Trust me! We are on top of it.

                    EVAN
          Really? Yesterday I was fatherless.
          Today, I have one, only to learn
          I'm about to lose him, too.
                    (pensive)
          --What I do understand is that he's
          all I've got left, and it seems to
          me that the longer I stay on the
          move, the longer he remains alive.

                    MANNINGTON
          Nonsense! I won't allow it!

                    EVAN
          I fear that's not your decision, sir.

     Evan rings off, takes a bite of a scone, gulps down some
     tea, slams money on the table and hurries for the door,
     where he stops, turns to the LANDLORD's wife.

                    EVAN
          Thank you, a lovely scone.

     She's too shy to respond.

                    LANDLORD
          Thank you, sir.

     Evan bolts out.

     EXT. LONDON STREET - DAY

     Evan quickly hails a taxi and jumps in.

                    EVAN
               (to Driver)
     Gatwick.

INT. HOLDING CELL - DAY

More hospital-like than jail cell, in the sterile room,
Rhodes, with cigar, sits on a cot as a SOLDIER arrives.

                    SOLDIER
               (thick Slavic accent)
     He want you.

                    RHODES
     Ah, lovely. I very much enjoy
     our stimulating conversations.

The expressionless soldier waves Rhodes out.

INT. KAZALI'S CHAMBER - DAY

The stark chamber appears NASA command center-like. Key
and circuitry boards, monitors abound. Oddly, two ornate
Toledo swords are proudly mounted on one wall.

Kazali savours a Puccini aria and a cigar from behind
his massive and gaudy, teak desk as Rhodes is delivered.

                    KAZALI
     Ah, my friend, how nice. Would you
     care for anything to drink?

                    RHODES
     You read my mind.

                    KAZALI
     Brandy okay?

                    RHODES
     When isn't it?

Kazali gestures for SOLDIER to fetch it.

                    KAZALI
     That's what I like about you,
     my friend. You are exceptionally
     well cultivated.

                    RHODES
That's quite the compliment.

                    KAZALI
Please, have a seat. I trust you
are finding the accommodations adequate?

                    RHODES
Absolutely. Modern minimalism with
careful consideration of Feng Shui.
I must ring my friends. They'd
really love to come pay you a visit.

As soldier delivers brandy, Kazali aims a remote at the
huge wall map. It splits in two, revealing a large TV.

                    KAZALI
We will talk about your friends
later. Right now, I thought you
would enjoy watching a rather
thrilling new video I have just
received. Would you mind?

                    RHODES
I love a good thriller.

Kazali starts the video. Nelly's cottage is on screen.

                    KAZALI
Isn't that stunning scenery?

Recognising the cottage, Rhodes tenses.

                    KAZALI (cont.)
Makes you wish you were there, no?

ON SCREEN, the silent video cuts to the cottage
interior. Nelly bound and gagged and seated on the sofa.

                    KAZALI (cont.)
This is my favourite part.

ON SCREEN, in a perverse harmony with the music in the
chamber, Nelly squirms, desperate to free herself.

Rhodes looks away, sees Kazali enjoying the video. Anger
swells in him and he begins to glare at Kazali.

ON SCREEN, the woman slowly suffocates.

                    KAZALI (cont.)
        Wow, now that is powerful.
        Wouldn't you agree?

Crushed, Rhodes is silent.

                    KAZALI (cont.)
        Would you care to see it again?

Rhodes springs upon him, but a soldier quickly clubs him
from behind, sending him to the floor. Kazali gloats.

                    KAZALI (cont.)
        Do my eyes deceive me, or has the
        Ever cool, calm and collected Evan
        Rhodes forgotten himself?
                    (to Soldier)
        Pick him up.

SOLDIER helps a wobbly Rhodes to his feet.

                    KAZALI (cont.)
                    (to Rhodes)
        It would appear you are mortal
        after all, my friend. Soon I
        shall show you just how mortal.
        But, before you embark upon that
        final voyage, there is another
        tour de force performance I
        plan to share with you.

Kazali grabs a photograph from his desk, holds it before
Rhodes. It's a shot of Evan riding his mountain bike.

                    KAZALI (cont.)
        Your son and the camera have a
        unique rapport, don't you think?

                    RHODES
        You bastard! He's done nothing.

                    KAZALI
        Come now, do not worry, I'm
        sure he will deliver a stellar
        performance.

                    RHODES
        He's a civilian, for Christ's sake.

                    KAZALI
        The Marquis of Queensbury rules
        are not applicable here. Anything
        and everything for the cause. You
        know this. You yourself have
        sacrificed wife and child for
        Queen and country. Have you not?

Rhodes' hateful glare is armour piercing.

                    KAZALI (cont.)
        Sacrifice, the price of our goals,
        the price of love. Love of country,
        love of family. ...Love is brutal, no?
                    (to soldier)
        Take him away.

As soldier hauls Rhodes out, Kazali puffs his cigar,
sips his brandy and joyfully sings along with the Puccini.

EXT. STREET OUTSIDE ATHENS AIRPORT - DAY

Evan emerges from the terminal and hails a taxi. In the
distance, a MAN in a white cotton suit, keeping a
watchful eye, dives into a waiting car.

A second MAN, wearing a matching white suit, waiting at
the wheel, hurries them off, after Evan's taxi.

EXT. STREET/ATHENS - DAY

Two taxis roll to a stop in front of the Hilton. Evan
jumps from one and enters the hotel. WHITE SUITS follow.

INT. HILTON HOTEL LOBBY/RECEPTION - DAY

The WHITE SUITS watch as Evan is led away by a BELLBOY.

INT. HOTEL CORRIDOR - DAY

As bellboy leads, Evan notices a beautiful, raven-haired
chambermaid, MICHELLE FOUCAT, 30, avoiding eye contact.
The instant the two men enter a room, she yanks out a
mobile phone from within her laundry trolley and dials.

EXT. RAILROAD BORDER CROSSING - DAY

A long train sits idling as uniformed Macedonian border
police inspect the train and its passengers' passports.

INT. TRAIN - DAY

TWO dark, burly MEN with thick mustaches, wearing RED
CROSS armbands, wait patiently as BORDER POLICE check
passports. MUSTACHE #1 glances out the window.

EXT. RAILROAD PLATFORM - DAY

A sign reads MACEDONIA. Several POLICEMEN gather about.
ONE looks back at Mustache #1 and subtly tips his hat.

INT. TRAIN - DAY

Police inspect "Mustache" passports and order them off.

EXT. TRAIN STATION - DAY

The "Mustaches" are led to a distant car in the long
line of connected passenger and cargo carriages.

Procession stops at a carriage surrounded by POLICEMEN.
The carriage door is slid open, revealing a dozen crates
stamped with the famous red cross.

Police review the manifest. There appears confusion.
HAT-TIPPER arrives, looks over the manifest, calmly
utters a few Macedonian words and all is settled.

Police shut up the carriage and disburse, HAT-TIPPER
returns the manifest, shares a smirk with the Mustaches.

EXT. ATHENS STREET/HILTON HOTEL - DAY

A lengthy queue of taxis waiting to collect fares in
front of the hotel. The DOORMAN hails one for Evan.
A taxi heading in the other direction makes a sharp U-
turn, cuts in front of the expected taxi, and stops
abruptly before Evan. DRIVER #1, livid, pops out,
cursing.

DRIVER #2, dressed in jeans, T-shirt, American baseball
cap, Michelle Foucat snaps back with equal fury.

Observing all from a distance, the WHITE SUITS share a
chuckle as a shocked Driver #1 retreats.

                    MICHELLE
              (French accent, to Evan)
        I am at your service, Monsieur.

> EVAN
> My, aren't we the eager beaver.

He slips into the taxi.

INT. TAXI - DAY

> EVAN
> The harbour, please.

Offering no response, she slides the window between them closed. The rear doors automatically CLICK locked.

Evan tries the doors. No use.

> EVAN (cont.)
> Professor-safe doors, eh?

Again, there is no reaction.

> EVAN (cont.)
> So, the hotel and the taxi?
> Gosh, tough times, eh? How
> many jobs do you have--

He spots road sign reading "AIRPORT 6K."

> EVAN (cont.)
> Hmm, somebody wants me out of
> Dodge. Mr. Rhumandi, I presume?

Suddenly, Michelle yanks opens the dividing window, angrily rips off her cap, and slams it onto the passenger seat.

> MICHELLE
> It is not wise to mention
> that name. It would mean much
> trouble for you.

> EVAN
> It already has.

> MICHELLE
> Yes, sadly, I know. But if that
> person should know you are in
> Athens, I would have been
> delivering your corpse to the
> airport. Understand?

                    EVAN
No, actually. I don't understand
any of this nightmare. Particularly
where you fit in.

                    MICHELLE
I am Michelle Foucat. I work
for the French government,
assigned to Athens.

                    EVAN
And it's your assignment to
drive me to the airport?

                    MICHELLE
What do you think you are
doing by coming here?

                    EVAN
Isn't it obvious? I'm hiding
in plain sight.

                    MICHELLE
Mr. Mannington is waiting for
you in London. It's much better
you leave this matter to him,
no? ...These killers, they are
the professionals.

                    EVAN
Professionals? Jesus! Why
flatter such psychopaths by
referring to them as "professional"?

                    MICHELLE
Despicable, yes! But they are
very good at what they do. I
understand how you feel, but--

                    EVAN
Do you?

She hesitates.

                    EVAN (cont.)
Connaissez-vous?

She falls silent and steers the taxi into the airport.

EXT. AIRPORT - DAY

Michelle pops out of the taxi, nods at two uniformed
SECURITY MEN awaiting her arrival. They rush to taxi.

> EVAN
> Friends of yours?

> MICHELLE
> They will see you to the plane.

The men arrive.

> MICHELLE (cont.)
> Truly, I am very sorry about your--

> EVAN
> Yes, well, fully functional
> families are such a bore, don't
> you think?

Michelle drops her head slightly, Evan quickly shoves,
her into the two men, then dives into the idling taxi.

> EVAN (cont.)
> Au re·voir, ma cheri.

He races off, leaving Michelle and company to dive into
a nearby security van and blast off after him.

EXT. ATHENS STREET - DAY

Evan weaves through the city traffic.

EXT. ANOTHER ATHENS STREET - DAY

The congestion is great, the obstacles numerous. Yet
Evan's taxi manages to dodge cars and avoid pedestrians.

INT. CAR - DAY

Adrenaline flows, yet Evan cracks a smile.

EXT. ANOTHER ATHENS STREET - DAY

As the security vehicle gaining, Evan makes a sharp
turn. For an instant the car is nearly on two wheels.

EXT. FIRST ATHENS STREET - DAY

The security car cannot manage the maneuver and
screeches and swerves to avoid striking pedestrians.

INT. CAR - DAY

Evan views success in the rearview mirror.

                    EVAN
        A bientot, ma cherie. A bientot.

INT. SECURITY CAR - DAY

Frustrated, the security men curse in Greek. Michelle
quietly collects herself. A thought occurs to her.

                    MICHELLE
        The harbour. Quickly!
                    (in Greek)
        The harbour!!!

The driver cranks the wheel and floors it.

INT. TAXI - DAY

The Athens street is bustling. Evan spots the French
embassy, parks in front and hops out.

EXT. ATHENS CITY STREET - DAY

A uniformed SECURITY OFFICER rushes out.

                    OFFICER
        You cannot park here!

                    EVAN
        Oh no, no. I'm not parking,
        I'm simply returning it.

He hands the officer the keys and hails another taxi.

                    OFFICER
        But, Monsieur?

                    EVAN
        No, no, no! It's my pleasure.
                    (climbing into taxi)
                    (MORE)

                         EVAN (cont.)
      Sorry, must dash.
                         (to driver)
      The harbour.

INT. UNDERGROUND FACILITY/SICK-ROOM - DAY

The sterile room is filled with cots. Most are empty.
The few disease-blotched patients are strapped in.

HAZMAT suits are standard issue. As TWO HAZMATS carry
out a body, Kazali surveys all with a prideful smile.

DR. VINCENT MARTINI, 45, biologist, appearing strained,
is led into the room by yet another SOLDIER.

                         KAZALI
      Ah, the good doctor. It appears
      you were right. With the addition
      of a simple enzyme, your strain
      has eliminated ninety-five percent
      of them in just two days. Well done!

Dr. Martini cannot bear to look.

                         KAZALI (cont.)
      I am most pleased. We must drink
      to your success when I return.

SOLDIER forcefully shoves Dr. Martini out. It brings a
smile to Kazali's face.

EXT. DOCK - ATHENS HARBOUR - DAY

Evan's taxi stops before the entrance to the dock.
Spotting the security van, Evan quickly jumps out and
shields himself behind a lorry. Peeking round, he spots
Michelle and SECURITY scanning the area.

Cargo is stacked everywhere. Using it as cover, Evan
creeps toward Michelle, before positioning himself
behind a crate.

As she searches, Evan waits, corners the crate, grabs
Michelle, quickly cupping one hand over her mouth.

                         EVAN
      Please forgive this most
                         (MORE)

                    EVAN (cont.)
     un-gentleman-like conduct. But
     it occurs to me you just might
     be able to assist me.

She squirms at the idea.

                    EVAN (cont.)
          Terribly sorry about your
          airport detail, but, I think it
          best I stay on the move.

Struggles to free herself is useless.

                    EVAN (cont.)
          So tell me, which craft belongs
          to this Rhumandi chap? --Look, I
          don't have much time. We're talking
          about Rhodes' life, for God's sake.

She relaxes. Evan is slow to trust her. She glares
reassurance and he cautiously releases her.

                    MICHELLE
          They are after you, as well.

                    EVAN
          Yes, well, who isn't, these days.

                    MICHELLE
          This is serious!

                    EVAN
          So am I!

                    MICHELLE
          This is not very wise.

                    EVAN
          Which is his boat?

                    MICHELLE
          You cannot walk up to Rhumandi,
          shake your fist in his face and
          state your demand. He is a killer,
          and he is very good at it.

                    EVAN
          Yes, I've seen his handiwork.

The remark softens her.

                    MICHELLE
          There is nothing you can do.

                    EVAN
          Hasn't it occurred to you lot
          that maybe Rhodes could shed some
          light on this bomb business?

                    MICHELLE
          Perhaps. But, there is nothing
          you can do on your own.

                    EVAN
          Then help me! You'll be surprised
          at what I'm capable of.

She hesitates, nervously looking over her shoulder.

                    MICHELLE
          Somehow, I do not think so.
          Besides, the boat it is not here.

Evan is about to challenge her statement, but she
continues before he can protest.

                    MICHELLE (cont.)
          The "La Dolce Far Niente" sailed to
          Corfu yesterday-- It is Carnivale.

                    EVAN
          If you know this psychopath's
          every move, why don't you just
          arrest him?

                    MICHELLE
          Rhumandi is not stupid. You will
          not catch him with the 'red-hand,'
          as you English say.

                    EVAN
          Welsh, actually--

                    MICHELLE
          Pardon?

                    EVAN
          How will I recognise him?

                        MICHELLE
No! It is too dangerous.

                        EVAN
What does the man look like?

                        MICHELLE
What is your plan?
(reads Evan's impatient face)
I have not seen him. Few people
have. But if you do find him,
you cannot mistake him. He will
be the tall Indian man with a
hole in the head.

                        EVAN
What?

                        MICHELLE
He has only one ear.

                        EVAN
Charming.
        (pecks her forehead)
Merci.

He dashes off carefully, yet the SECURITY MEN spot him
and a chase over, through and around crates ensues,
spilling over a few crates in the process.

DOCKWORKERS are irate. Close to reaching his waiting
taxi, a WORKER angrily swings a crowbar at Evan. He
ducks and quickly counters with a stiff punch.

Evan swiftly grabs the crowbar, punctures a tire on the
security car, before diving into his waiting taxi.

INT. TAXI - DAY

                        EVAN
    Go!

EXT. CORFU TOWN'S NEW PORT - DAY

A crowd of tourists explodes off a large inter-island
ferry. Evan, amongst them, scans the area as he
disembarks and makes his way to the nearby public beach.

Evan's path is hampered by a mass of sun worshippers
filled with Carnivale spirit, an epidemic of merriment.

In between the multitude of singing and dancing bodies,
Evan spots the "La Dolce Far Niente" in the harbour.

He makes his way onto the public beach. To blend in with
the crowd, he removes his shirt, shoes and trousers,
revealing a pair of swimming trunks.

He places his items into a plastic bag and seals it,
then steps into the ocean. Once in the water, he ties
the bag to his ankle, before swimming toward the yacht.

EXT. CORFU AIRPORT - DAY

As a small plane lands, a posh SUV hurries to meet it.
Kazali and a buxom COMPANION emerge. He pats her bottom,
climbs into the SUV, leaving her with plane and crew.

EXT. CORFU TOWN HARBOUR - DAY

The SUV weaves through the unleashed street mirth,
before stopping at a small dock. Kazali and a swarthy,
DRIVER exit, board a moored speedboat, then speed away.

EXT. CORFU TOWN HARBOUR/SEA - DAY

Nearing the vessel, Evan slips underwater, where he
removes his plastic bag and ties it to the anchor cable
of a nearby yacht, then slowly surfaces.

INT. LA DOLCE FAR NIENTE - DAY

The cabin is palatial, a gigantic TV, the focal point.

ON SCREEN is RHUMANDI, 60, a stick of a man, seated
between two voluptuous WOMEN. His sinister face, stern
manner and hideously disgusting, hairy stump for a right
ear come across loud and clear.

SLATOVAK, 50, an equally menacing looking Romanian man,
stands at attention video-conferencing with an enraged
Rhumandi. Another BUXOM WOMAN sits watching events.

                    RHUMANDI
          Where is the boy now?

>   SLATOVAK
>   We do not yet know, Excellency.
>
>   RHUMANDI
>   What about the Parakeet?
>
>   SLATOVAK
>   He does not know, Excellency.
>
>   RHUMANDI
>   Why not? What do we pay him for?
>
>   SLATOVAK
>   The young man is no longer in the
>   hands of the British government.
>
>   RHUMANDI
>   How difficult can it be to
>   locate some schoolmaster? --I
>   trust I do not have to remind
>   you of the penalty for failure?
>
>   SLATOVAK
>   No, Excellency! --I do it myself.
>
>   RHUMANDI
>   Make this young educator's
>   "disciplinary action" a slow
>   and brutally painful one.
>
>   SLATOVAK
>   Of course, Excellency.

EXT. CORFU TOWN HARBOUR - DAY

As Evan begins to scale the ship side, he spots Kazali's
speedboat racing toward the La Dolce Far Niente and
quickly sinks back into the water.

Only eyes above the water, Evan watches Kazali step from
the speedboat onto the larger vessel. Once the brute is
aboard Evan carefully scales the boat's side.

INT. LA DOLCE FAR NIENTE - DAY

>   RHUMANDI
>   Ah, Captain Kazali, I trust
>   you have good news for me.

                    KAZALI
        Yes, Excellency. Certainly.

                    RHUMANDI
                    (to Slatovak)
        This man who knows how to crack
        the whip.
                    (to Kazali)
        You must instruct Mr. Slatovak
        in the fine art of instilling
        the drive for success in his men.

                    KAZALI
        I would be delighted.

                    RHUMANDI
        Now, how is our little enterprise?

                    KAZALI
        Very well, Excellency. Very
        well, indeed.

EXT. DECK/LA DOLCE FAR NIENTE - DAY

Evan sneaks, following the sound of voices. Successfully
avoiding being seen by DECK HANDS, he spots a porthole
and cautiously peers in.

INT. LA DOLCE FAR NIENTE - DAY

Kazali glances about the room.

                    KAZALI
        May we speak freely, Excellency?

                    RHUMANDI
        My dear Captain, the 'La Dolce'
        emits radio-wave interference
        to scramble all transmissions.
        Our Western eavesdroppers are
        mere stone age fumblers.
                    (gestures for Kazali to continue)
        Please.

                    KAZALI
        My men with the Albanian and
        Macedonian customs have seen to
        it that our cargo has successfully
                    (MORE)

                    KAZALI (cont.)
        crossed into Romania, where
        Slatovak's men will make certain
        it crosses into Hungary unmolested.

                    RHUMANDI
                    (to Slatovak)
        I trust these men are reliable?

                    SLATOVAK
        Yes, Excellency, yes.

                    RHUMANDI
        For your sake, they had better be.

He signals to Kazali to continue.

                    KAZALI
        The cargo will arrive in Budapest
        tomorrow evening, under British
        and American surveillance-- I
        shall meet the freight, which
        should further fuel allied
        speculation.
                    RHUMANDI
        Excellent! And our other diversions?

                    KAZALI
        A squadron in each location has
        been deployed.

MONTAGE

New York City street. Three uniformed CUSTODIANS,
toolboxes in hand, exit a van and stride into the
Chrysler Building.

                    KAZALI (V.O.)
        They have been instructed to
        imply be conspicuous. That is all.

Chicago street. Three uniformed CUSTODIANS, with
toolboxes, exit a van and enter the Willis Tower.

Madrid street. Three uniformed CUSTODIANS, with
toolboxes, enter the Museo del Prado.

END MONTAGE

INT. LA DOLCE FAR NIENTE - DAY

>   RHUMANDI
>   And how are we progressing at Wooge?

>   KAZALI
>   We have only to wait on the weather.

>   RHUMANDI
>   And our good friend Mr. Rhodes?

>   KAZALI
>   Never has a man enjoyed himself more.

>   RHUMANDI
>   You have performed exceptionally.
>   (to Slatovak)
>   Learn much from our comrade.

EXT. DECK/LA DOLCE FAR NIENTE - DAY

Evan mouths the word "wooge" as he ponders its meaning.

INT. LA DOLCE FAR NIENTE - DAY

As Slatovak sulks, Kazali hands DVD to the buxom woman.

>   KAZALI
>   My masterpiece, Excellency.

>   RHUMANDI
>   Ah! I wish I had been there to see
>   the expression on Mr. Rhodes' face.

>   KAZALI
>   If you please, Excellency, I
>   have included that on the tape.

>   RHUMANDI
>   My dear Capitan, you honour me.

>   KAZALI
>   The honour is all mine, Excellency.

EXT. DECK/LA DOLCE FAR NIENTE - DAY

A DECKHAND discovers Evan, rips a mounted fire ax from
the wall and charges. Evan bobs, weaves, and a battle
for the ax ensues. The commotion alerts all aboard.

INT. LA DOLCE FAR NIENTE - DAY

                    RHUMANDI (ON SCREEN)
     What is that?

                    KAZALI
     One moment, Excellency.

Kazali and Slatovak rush out.

EXT. DECK/LA DOLCE FAR NIENTE - DAY

The ax narrowly misses Evan, so he kicks his man into
the deck rail and follows with a body combination.

                    EVAN
     What say we bury the hatchet?

As Evan sends the brute overboard with a right cross,
DECKHANDS arrive. Evan quickly dives into the sea, as
the deck-hands fire wildly into the water at him.

EXT. IONIAN SEA/UNDERWATER - DAY

Short of breath, Evan hurriedly swims for another boat.

EXT. DECK/LA DOLCE FAR NIENTE - DAY

Kazali and Slatovak arrive on deck.

                    KAZALI
     Cease firing!

The gunfire quickly stops.

                    DECKHAND #2
     An intruder, Capitan.

                    KAZALI
     Do not bother.

                    DECKHAND
     But, Capitan--

                    KAZALI
     Did you not hear me? Idiot! What
     else have they to do? They grasp
     at straws. They know nothing. Do
     you wish to give the impression
     we have something to hide?

                    DECKHAND #2
    No, Capitan.

                    KAZALI
        Idiot!

Kazali and Slatovak storm off.

EXT. IONIAN SEA/UNDERWATER - DAY

Evan retrieves his gear from the cable. He then
hurriedly swims for another boat. Using the boat as
cover, he surfaces.

INT. LA DOCE FAR NIENTE - DAY

Kazali and Slatovak return to the cabin.

                    RHUMANDI
        What is happening?

                    KAZALI
        It is nothing, Excellency. Only
        our curious little friends.

                    RHUMANDI
        Excellent! It would appear they
        have taken the bait. --Well done,
        gentlemen. I leave you to it, then.

Kazali and Slatovak bow and march out.

EXT. DECK/LA DOLCE FAR NIENTE - DAY

Kazali and Slatovak board a launch and speed away.

EXT. IONIAN SEA - DAY

Evan ties bag to his ankle and swims back to the beach.

EXT. PUBLIC BEACH - DAY

Evan emerges from the sea, drops to the sand to collect
himself. Yet, Michelle's voice drops from the heavens.

                    MICHELLE (O.S.)
        So, this is your plan?

Evan turns to find Michelle's long, lovely legs before
him. Binoculars in hand; a mobile phone is hooked to the
top of her painfully sexy mini-sport-shorts.

                    MICHELLE (cont.)
          C'est une bonne idee, if you
          plan to let Kazali get away.

                    EVAN
          What do you know about that chap?

                    MICHELLE
          Only that he is an arms dealer,
          a mercenary, a killer for hire,
          and an extortionist.

                    EVAN
          Your typical over achiever, eh?

                    MICHELLE
          It was Kazali who captured your
          Monsieur Rhodes in Algeria.

                    EVAN
          I don't suppose you know where
          they've taken him?

                    MICHELLE
          Regretfully, no.

Unconvinced, Evan hurries to dress.

                    EVAN
          What do you know about wooge?

                    MICHELLE
          Comment?

                    EVAN
          Look, I've really enjoyed our
          little chat, but I'm afraid I--

                    MICHELLE
          Kazali has got away. How do you
          intend to find him without me?

                    EVAN
          I thought you wanted me out of it?

                    MICHELLE
It would be safer for you, yes.
But, I would not wish to see such
a nice person
                (scans his physique)
bruised in any way.

                    EVAN
Thanks, but I have a plane to catch.

                    MICHELLE
Ah, you have something maybe I
think. Your little plan was not
such the failure after all, no?
Maybe I can help.

                    EVAN
Thanks, but I'm afraid Budapest
is a little out of your reach.

                    MICHELLE
I have longer reach than you think.

                    EVAN
Yes, you are rather lanky.

                    MICHELLE
Well, since the scenery agrees with
you, we should attend Carnivale, no?

                    EVAN
I'd love to, but, as I said--

                    MICHELLE
It is Carnivale. Kazali will not
leave until the morning. So, we
have the chance to keep the
eye on him.

                    EVAN
How do you know he hasn't
already left the island?

                    MICHELLE
As I said, I have quite the reach.

EXT. STREET - DAY

Evan follows Michelle to yet another taxi.

                         EVAN
        You're really a cabby, aren't you?

                       MICHELLE
        It would be safer for us, no?

                         EVAN
        I'm not sure, I've seen you drive.

She ignores the remark. They climb in car.

INT. TAXI - DAY

                         EVAN
        Where to?

                       MICHELLE
        We can stay at a friend's house.
        You will be safe there.

                         EVAN
        I'm looking for Kazali, not a
        hiding place.

                       MICHELLE
        You are very much silly. He will
        kill you the second he sets the
        eye on you.

                         EVAN
        This friend of yours, he isn't
        one of your security chums,
        ready to ship me off to London?

                       MICHELLE
        No, she is not. Besides, she is
        in Paris at the moment. Do not
        worry, no one will bother you there.

                         EVAN
        Hmmm, pity.

INT. FRIEND'S APARTMENT - DAY

Entering, Evan surveys the stylish flat.

                       MICHELLE
        It is a lovely place to hide, no?

EVAN
You must remind me to cower more
often. I hear women find that
extremely appealing in a man.

MICHELLE
You are very ridiculous, yes?

EVAN
Speaking of ridiculous, I don't
exactly imagine we'll find Kazali
dancing naked in the street tonight.

MICHELLE
It would be funny, yes?

EVAN
Perish the thought.

MICHELLE
He will be at the Casino, as usual.
But you cannot go without the
proper attire-- I'll take care
of it, after I find us some food.

EVAN
Food, clothes, lodging? You're
turning out to be quite--

MICHELLE
Do not think I help because you
are handsome, yes? I am very
good at my job.

EVAN
I'm keenly aware of that.

MICHELLE
My friends, who have served in
the wars, suffer the maladies of
the desert. But more than that,
it is my uncle Pablo, my mother's
brother, he worked for the Spanish
government. He was with Rhodes--

EVAN
I should like to meet your uncle,
my Spanish luv.

MICHELLE
He is dead. They kill him the
night they took your Monsieur Rhodes.

EVAN
I'm so sorry.

MICHELLE
I loved him very-- So, I am here
keeping the eye on Rhumani's men.

EVAN
Why Greece?

MICHELLE
We are watching the Albanian border.

EVAN
Albania?

MICHELLE
Oui. It is difficult to get the
permission to cross the border,
yet Rhumandi's men come and go
as they wish --Now hurry, we
have much to do.

INT. TAXI - NIGHT

Michelle and Evan, in black tie, are the epitome of the
elegant couple. In contrast to her stunning beauty,
Michelle surprises Evan by pulling a small pistol from
her handbag and hands it to him.

MICHELLE
In case there is the trouble.

EVAN
How thoughtful, but no.

MICHELLE
Kazali is a killer.

EVAN
Yes, but I'm not.

MICHELLE
You teach the boxing and fencing, no?

                    EVAN
          Disciplines, luv, disciplines.

                    MICHELLE
          Disciplines?

                    EVAN
          A tool. Something used to hone
          mind and body. But, violence?
          Never! That's for the foolish
          and the simple-minded.

                    MICHELLE
          You want to put your head in the
          lion's mouth without the whip?
          Now, that is foolish.

                    EVAN
          The trick is in never letting
          the lion sense you fear him.

Frustrated, Michelle slips the gun back into her bag.

EXT. CASINO - CORFU TOWN - NIGHT

Michelle and Evan emerge from the taxi and weave through
the joyous, semi-naked island populace, to the casino.

INT. CASINO FOYER - NIGHT

The elegant, dignified foyer reveals it as the only spot
in the city uninfected by the Carnivale merriment.

As Evan and Michelle enter, a DOORMAN slyly places an
item in her hand and whispers in her ear.

                    EVAN
          A friend of yours?

She produces a pair of Buddy Holly glasses.

                    MICHELLE
          Put these on.

                    EVAN
          You're joking?

                    MICHELLE
          We cannot take the chance.

>   EVAN
>   This is your idea of a disguise?

>   MICHELLE
>   Do you wish my help or not?

As Evan reluctantly slips on the specs, Michelle quickly
sticks the mustache on him, then musses his hair.

>   EVAN
>   Happy now?

>   MICHELLE
>   Oui, I am very much happier.

>   EVAN
>   Yes, I can tell.

>   MICHELLE
>   You look very dashing.

>   EVAN
>   Yes, I understand the librarian
>   look is all the rage. By the
>   way, how did you manage
>   (re: tuxedo)
>   such a perfect fit?

With a quick survey of his body and a deep sigh, she
takes his hand and leads him into the casino.

INT - CASINO - NIGHT

The opulent room is packed with exquisitely garbed
patrons. Money, like cigar smoke is everywhere. Kazali,
is child-like, as roulette ball lands on his number.

As Michelle and Evan watch from afar, a SERVER with tray
of drinks arrives.

>   SERVER
>   Chateau d'Yquem?

>   EVAN
>   Ah, my saviour.
>   (to Michelle re: Kazali)
>   That is the evil mastermind?
>   He behaves like a child.

MICHELLE
Do you English never let down
the hair?

EVAN
English?

MICHELLE
Ah, yes. How you say, Abber-reest-weeth?

EVAN
Read up on me, I see.

MICHELLE
Of course.

EVAN
It's Wales, not England!

MICHELLE
Is the same thing, no?

EVAN
Like Belgium is France?

Michelle's protest is a mere chuckle.

MICHELLE
I also read that you have no
lover at the moment. Yes?

EVAN
That depends upon which moment
you refer to?

MICHELLE
You know, I once met Monsieur Rhodes
in Paris. Very much the handsome man.
It is easy to see why your mother--
                    (takes his hand)
I'm sorry.

EVAN
Yes, perhaps there really is no
such thing as happily ever after.

MICHELLE
No! It is rare, yes? But I
believe many people do find it.

                    EVAN
        You're awfully optimistic for a spy.

                    MICHELLE
        You are too pessimistic for the
        idealistic university professor, no?

                    EVAN
        ReallY? --Got a pen?

                    MICHELLE
        Comment?

                    EVAN
        A pen! ...Un stylo?

She produces a fountain pen from her bag. He grabs it
and starts for the roulette table. She grabs his arm.

                    MICHELLE
        What do you think you are doing?

                    EVAN
        Being optimistic!!

He pulls away and strides toward Kazalil.

INT. CASINO - ROULETTE TABLE - NIGHT

TWO THUGS stand watch over Kazali playing. Reaching the
table, Evan plants himself.

                    EVAN
            (to croupier, in American accent)
        Two hundred Euro, please.

Kazali and the other gamblers take no notice of Evan
until he takes pad and pen from his jacket, makes a
calculation, then places a winning bet.

Evan repeats the approach with methodical precision and
wins again. Curious, Kazali moves over for a closer look.

                    KAZALI
        Excuse me, but I could not help
        notice your great skill, Monsieur.

Evan plays mildly-aloof-scientist.

                    EVAN
What? --Oh, no, sir. I assure you,
this won't continue for very much
longer. Like any other game of
chance, the trick is knowing when
to walk away.

                    KAZALI
You calculate when to walk away?

                    EVAN
In a manner of speaking, yes.

Choosing not to elaborate, Evan checks his figures. Both
place bets. Only Evan wins.

                    KAZALI
How, might I ask, did you chance
upon such a winning theory, sir?

                    EVAN
Not much chance in it, really.

                    KAZALI
Really? Enlighten me, if you would.

                    EVAN
I'm an engineer you see-- Anyway,
it came to me that a schematic
based on linear equations, which
are the very foundation of
probability, might-- Well, you
take the notion of chance, factor
in the square root of the binary
form of the number 4700 and divide
that number by the last winning
number on the wheel-- Oh, excuse
me, I'm running on again.

                    KAZALI
Not at all. Fascinating! I admit,
I am no mathematician. Fascinating,
nonetheless. Please, permit me to
buy you a drink.

                    EVAN
I'd enjoy that immensely. But this
is the first vacation my wife and
I have had in 9 years. I'm afraid--

                    KAZALI
    Surely your wife would understand.
    I am always looking for a better
    system. I cannot stand to lose.

                    EVAN
    I quite understand. Unfortunately--
            (collects winnings)
    Wooge you believe this?

                    KAZALI
    What did you say?

                    EVAN
    Excuse me?

                    KAZALI
    Just now, I didn't quite catch that.

As Evan slides chips to CROUPIER, Kazali studies him.

                    EVAN
    Would you believe how much I've
    won here? Tess, that's my wife,
    will be very pleased I didn't
    lose my shirt on one of my hair
    brained theories.
            (to croupier)
    Will you cash these, please?
            (to Kazali)
    Well, good night to you.

As Evan walks back to a nervous Michelle, a pensive
Kazali, signals VIKTOR, 35, a massive thug, to follow.

                    MICHELLE
    Just what do you think you do?

                    EVAN
    Testing the waters, so to speak.

INT. CASINO FOYER - NIGHT

Evan and Michelle hurry through the foyer.

                    MICHELLE
    It was a mistake to come here.
            (to Doorman)
    Let me know if we are followed.

58

EXT. CASINO FOYER - NIGHT

Viktor watches Michelle rush Evan into a waiting taxi.

INT. TAXI - NIGHT

                    MICHELLE
          You are reckless.

                    EVAN
          A tad impatient, perhaps.

                    MICHELLE
          What was it you swimming for, then?
          What? Why do you risk our lives?

                    EVAN
          I had a plan.

                    MICHELLE
          Your plan is to be killed?

                    EVAN
          Wooge.

                    MICHELLE
          Wooge? What? What is this wooge?

                    EVAN
          I'm not sure.

                    MICHELLE
          No, I do not care for your plans.

INT. CASINO - NIGHT

Viktor returns to Kazali.

                    VIKTOR
          The wife I have seen before,
          I think.

                    KAZALI
          Interesting.

The ball lands on Kazali's number.

                    KAZALI (cont.)
          Theories, indeed.

EXT. STREET - CORFU TOWN - NIGHT

Evan and Michelle climb out of the taxi and make their
way to the apartment. Michelle nervously scans the area.

INT. FRIEND'S APARTMENT - NIGHT

Evan and Michelle enter. Relieved, she drops her wrap on
the sofa. Evan heads to the bookcase.

>   MICHELLE
>   I cannot believe-- Right under the
>   nose, you flaunt yourself and still
>   they do not notice. Either you have
>   the luck or something is wrong, I
>   think. --What did he say?

>   EVAN
>   He wanted to know how I managed it.

>   MICHELLE
>   What?

He drops a large stack of money on the dining table,
which renders her speechless.

>   EVAN
>   Marvelous affect money has on women.

>   MICHELLE
>   Combien?

>   EVAN
>   Oh, about thirty thousand.

>   MICHELLE
>   Pounds? --How do you do this?

>   EVAN
>   I'll be damned if I know. Now,
>   what's there to drink in this place?

She searches through a large antique bureau.

>   MICHELLE
>   Yes, it is definitely the luck.
>   There is only the pedestrian retsina
>   or a Chateaux Margeaux 95, but I
>   think my friend, maybe she save
>   this one for the special occasion?

                    EVAN
        Did we not just put our heads into
        the lion's mouth and come away unscathed?

                    MICHELLE
        You're right. It is the special
        occasion, a very special occasion.

                    EVAN
        Ah, a woman after my own heart.

As she retrieves the wine and two glasses from the
bureau, she notices Evan browsing through the bookshelf.

                    MICHELLE
        And what is it you look for?

                    EVAN
        An atlas. A map or something.

                    MICHELLE
        Pourquoi?

                    EVAN
        Wooge.

                    MICHELLE
        Again this wooge? What is this wooge?

                    EVAN
        I'm not sure. I'm guessing it's
        where Kazali has stashed Rhodes?

                    MICHELLE
        Why did you not tell me this before?

                    EVAN
        Until tonight, I wasn't sure of
        anything-- Except maybe one thing.

                    MICHELLE
        What is that?

                    EVAN
        You're superb.

                    MICHELLE
        You say this to all les cabbies, no?

                    EVAN
        Only those wear dresses like that.

He kisses her softly, then again, and again.

                  MICHELLE
        Hmmm, the Abber-reest-weeth kiss.

After another gentle kiss, he swoops her up and carries
her into the bedroom.

EXT. TRAIN STATION/BORDER CROSSING - NIGHT

The train rolls to a stop before several POLICEMEN.
Slatovak watches from the platform.

INT. TRAIN - NIGHT

As POLICE examine passports, Mustache #1 peers out the
window. The Police follow suit. Slatovak's presence on
the platform means everything. Police leave.

INT. MICHELLE'S BEDROOM - DAY BREAK

Faint sunlight struggles in through the curtains. Evan
and Michelle are woken by the phone. Michelle answers.

                  MICHELLE
        Allo...Oui...Quand? ...Oui, maintenant!

She slams down the phone.

                MICHELLE (cont.)
        Quickly, Evan. Quickly!

                    EVAN
        What's the matter?

                  MICHELLE
        Kazali's plane has just taken off.

                    EVAN
        I thought your man was watching him?

They scramble to dress.

                  MICHELLE
        What is he to do? Ask him to wait
                  (MORE)

                    MICHELLE (cont.)
        so we can follow? No! --It is okay.
        We have scheduled a courier flight
        to stop in Budapest.

                    EVAN
        When?

                    MICHELLE
        It leaves in forty minutes.

        She scribbles a note and hands it to him.

                    MICHELLE (cont.)
        This is the name of a friend in
        Budapest. --You see, my reach is
        much longer than you think, no?

                    EVAN
        Yes, so I've discovered.

        EXT. FRIEND'S APARTMENT - DAY BREAK

        Rushing out the apartment door, Evan and Michelle are
        met by the WHITE SUITES: JOHNSON and MURPHY, both 40.

                    MURPHY
        Mr. Rhodes?

                    EVAN
        Tydfil.

                    MICHELLE
        They are the American CIA.

                    MURPHY
                    (flashes ID)
        You are correct, Ms. Foucat.
                    (to Evan)
        We've been asked by your government--

                    EVAN
                    (to Michelle)
        I thought we had a deal? I hideout
        here, under your-- But all along,
        you were planning to send me back?

                    MICHELLE
What do you talk of? I do not--

                     EVAN
You lying cow! You just can't
play around with people's lives!

                    MURPHY
Take it easy, Mr. Rho--

Evan quickly punches and drops him. Johnson is instantly
upon him, but Evan surprises him with a flurry that
drops Johnson, as well.

                     EVAN
Tydfil! The name's Tydfil!

Murphy starts to regain himself and Evan quickly tags
him again, then quickly takes the dazed men's guns.

Evan plants a kiss on Michelle's cheek.

                  EVAN (cont.)
Sorry to leave you to tidy up
here. You'll be all right?

Michelle hands over the taxi keys.

                    MICHELLE
My associate waits for you at the
Package Express hanger. Bon chance!

Evan kisses her, then dives into the taxi and races off.

EXT. PACKAGE EXPRESS HANGER - DAY

The taxi screeches to a halt. Michelle's casino DOORMAN
and jet stand ready. Evan jumps from the taxi.

                    DOORMAN
He has one hour head start.

He extends a flat hand with handgun on it.

                     EVAN
Oh, God, no! In fact, take these.

He pulls CIA guns out of his jacket and hands them to
DOORMAN, then rushes aboard the plane.

EXT. 10 DOWNING STREET - DAY

Mannington emerges from a posh, dark car. Surrounded by
agents and police, he enters the building.

INT. 10 DOWNING/PM'S OFFICE - DAY

Nervously pacing like a first-time-father-to-be, PRIME
MINISTER, 65, greets Mannington as he enters.

                    PRIME MINISTER
          Have the Americans turned up anything?

                    MANNINGTON
          Nothing, sir.

                    PRIME MINISTER
          Damn! And what about the Rhodes boy?

                    MANNINGTON
          So far, sir, he has managed to elude
          the French, the Greeks, the American
          CIA, and Rhumandi's men.

                    PRIME MINISTER
          Quite a lad. But we cannot have him
          mucking up our entire operation. Get
          your desk jockeys out in the field.
          I want that Rhumandi bastard's head.
          An ear won't cut it this time--
          We've only four days left.

                    MANNINGTON
          Yes, sir.

INT. FERIHEY AIRPORT - BUDAPEST - DAY

Evan heads to a public telephone. In the distance a
slight, meek, MILO KIRLCH, 40, watches his every move.

Evan digs out Michelle's contact's number. Dialing, he
spots Milo's reflection in the surrounding glass. After
a few rings, he makes for the exit.

EXT. BUDAPEST STREET - DAY

Evan casually rounds a corner of the terminal building
and waits. The instant Milo appears Evan grabs him by
the collar and shoves him against the wall.

                    MILO
    No, Mr. Rhodes, please!

                    EVAN
    What do you want?

                    MILO
    Please, Mr. Rhodes, I am Milo.
    Michelle's friend. I am here to--

                    EVAN
    Tydfil. My name is Tydfil. Evan
    Tydfil. Got it? --Are you Kirlch?

Milo nods confirmation.

                    EVAN (cont.)
    What are you tailing me for? I
    was supposed to ring you.

                    MILO
    I thought it easier-- I have a car.

Milo points to a very old and extremely battered Lada
parked nearby. It doesn't inspire confidence.

                    MILO (cont.)
    It is the only car I have ever
    owned. It is very reliable.

Evan rolls his eyes, as they climb in.

INT. CAR - DAY

                    MILO
    The Americans, the British and my
    government are all watching Kazali.

                    EVAN
    And just where, exactly, is all this
    'watching' taking place?

                    MILO
    The train station. He is there.

                    EVAN
    Let's go.

EXT. TRAIN STATION - DAY

Kazali meets with "Mustaches". Together they examine the
contents of a cargo carriage. In the distance, a hidden
allied group of AGENTS watch with binoculars.

ANNA KOVACS, 32, Hungarian version of the quintessential
Hitchcockian-ice-cold-blonde, and STYLES, 40, more IBM
executive than MI6 agent, head the GROUP.

INT. MILO'S CAR - DAY

                    EVAN
          Come on, let's get going.

Milo hands a folded map to Evan.

                    MILO
          Michelle say you look for wooge?

                    EVAN
     Yes!

                    MILO
          It is a city. In the English it
          is Lodz. But, in the Polish, it
          is Wooge. On the way to Warsaw
          you will reach Lodz first.

                    EVAN
          --I've got a train to catch, then.

EXT. TRAIN STATION - DAY

KARL, 40, a Hungarian Jake Web, Anna and Styles watching
Kazali and his men, spot Milo's car entering the car park.

                    STYLES
          Like a Swiss watch, right on time.

                    ANNA
          Shame you will have to take him
          to London. He is rather handsome.

                    STYLES
          Sorry, but orders-is-orders.

INT. CAR - DAY

Evan is poised to spring out.

                    MILO
     Wait!

He retrieves a gun from under his seat.

                    MILO (cont.)
          Just in the case?

                    EVAN
          What? No! Why is a gun the first
          thing you people think of? --No!

Milo pulls out a thin, pencil-like knife with wrist
strap, from his jacket pocket.

                    MILO
          Then you take this? You wear it
          on wrist, under the sleeve--

                    EVAN
          No! --I thought you're in research?

Milo pulls a wristwatch from his pocket.

                    MILO
          Now, please, at least take this.

                    EVAN
          I've got a watch.

                    `MILO
          Yes, but not like this.

He sets on a small laser beam with the watch, briefly
burning the car's already worn carpeting.

                    EVAN
          What nightmare have I stepped into?

                    MILO
     Please.

                    EVAN
          Okay! Just the watch, mind you.

                    MILO
          --You also have Michelle's pen, yes?

                    EVAN
          I what? --How did you know?

                    MILO
          Give to me, please.

Evan pulls the pen from his pocket and hands it to him.

                    MILO (cont.)
          You must be very careful with
          this. The nib is sharp like the
          razor and weighted for the
          throwing. Inside is mixture of
          ordinary ink and curare, a poison
          that produces instant death.

                    EVAN
          Ah, lovely. Return it to her for me.

Milo slips the pen into Evan's breast pocket.

                    MILO
          I'm afraid she insists you keep it.
          --Now, we get you to the train.

But his door won't open. It's blocked by Anna and Karl.
Evan's by Styles. Anna taps on the window.

INT/EXT. CAR/STREET - DAY

                    ANNA
          It is awfully rude not to introduce
          me to your handsome friend, Milo.

Milo nervously cranks the down the window.

                    ANNA (cont.)
          Hello, Mr. Rhodes. I am Annoka
          Kovacs, but I go by Anna. Like
          Milo, I too work for the Hungarian
          government-- I see you have met
          my friend.
                    (re: Styles)
          Like you, he too is from England.

Evan is about to correct her when--

                    STYLES
     I must ask you to come--

                    EVAN
     You spooks are like broken records.

                    ANNA
     I understand your concern for your
     father, but you cannot interfere--

                    EVAN
     Oh, no! You misunderstand. I
     wouldn't dream of raining on
     your parade. I'm just an
     average tourist on holiday.

                    ANNA
     You do not look very average to me.
          (to Styles)
     We shall take Mr. Rhodes--

                    EVAN
     Tydfil.

                    ANNA
     Mr. Tydfil to the Kempinski Hotel,
     a guest of my government-- He will
     be quite safe. I shall keep the
     constant eye on him.
          (to Milo)
     Out! I shall drive.

Milo climbs out and into the rear seat. Styles joins him
as Anna positions herself behind the wheel.

                    ANNA (cont.)
          (to Karl)
     Call if Kazali even scratches himself.

She stamps down on the peddle, thrusting all backward.

INT. CAR - DAY

                    ANNA
     Planning a trip, Milo, yes?

                    EVAN
     Mr. Kirlch offered to translate--

                    ANNA
          Yes, Milo is a very generous man.
                    (to Milo)
          --Aren't you, Milo?

Milo, trembling, is unable to answer.

                    ANNA (cont.)
          He is also modest. --Like Milo,
          I would like to assist you, but
          our orders are not to confront
          the enemy until the train arrives
          in Vienna.

                    EVAN
          Vienna?

                    ANNA
          Yes, the train, it goes to Vienna.
          Where did you think it was to go?
          There is something you wish to share?

                    EVAN
          Yes, you handle this car very well.

                    ANNA
          You think it strange for a woman--

                    EVAN
          I find it most exhilarating.

She looks him up and down.

                    ANNA
          Difficult things are my speciality.

EXT. TRAIN STATION - NIGHT

Karl and group observe Kazali disembark from the train.
As it clears the platform, sight of Kazali's obstructed.
When the train rolls on, the platform is empty. Karl
immediately yanks out his mobile and dials.

INT. EVAN'S SUITE/KEMPINKSI HOTEL - NIGHT

The suite is fit for a king. Anna ushers in ROOM SERVICE
with a trolley filled with culinary delights. Styles
jabbers on his phone. Petrified Milo sits nervously.

Evan peeks out a window. There's no escape.

> ANNA
> (to Evan)
> Ah! Now this is food. Not that
> dog meal you eat in England, yes?

Phone rings. She waves the server out as she answers.

> ANNA (cont.)
> Yes, yes, he is here ...Yes, I
> shall inform him.

She disconnects and looks to Styles.

> ANNA
> The train, it has departed. But
> there is no sign of Kazali.

> STYLES
> What do you mean, no sign of him?

> ANNA
> Apparently, we will now have to
> add magician to his dossier--
> Now, go! I shall stay here and
> keep watch over our detainee—
> Have Milo returned to the wife.
> (to Milo)
> We shall speak of your part in
> this later.

Styles steers Milo out.

> EVAN
> Detainee? Next, you'll have me
> in chains.

> ANNA
> That would be tremendous fun,
> no? But first, you must eat.
> You need your strength.

She reaches for the wine bottle on trolley.

> EVAN
> Allow me.

ANNA
So, chivalry is not dead in
Britain, then?

EVAN
Never! It's the essence of a
knight's fabric.

ANNA
The knights are all gone, no?

EVAN
Never! We've incredible endurance.

ANNA
Hmmm, lovely.

EXT. POLISH COUNTRYSIDE - NIGHT

The richly black sky of the lonely countryside is ruined
by the lights, noise and wind of a helicopter landing.

Kazali, Slatovak and Viktor climb out of the chopper and
rush to a dilapidated large wooden BARN and march in.

INT. BARN - NIGHT

Empty, save for dried straw, the barn is a ghost town.
High in a corner a camouflaged camera is mounted.

KAZALI
(into camera)
Engage lift.

POV - CAMERA.

Infrared: Kazali, Slatovak and Viktor.

END POV

A sudden noise accompanies the lowering of the straw
covered ground. It and the men sink into the earth.

INT. - UNDERGROUD FACILITY - NIGHT

The lift bottoms out and Kazali, Slatovak and Viktor
step off. The large, stark, sterile facility is a myriad
of corridors, packed with busy SOLDIERS.

INT. KEMPINSKI HOTEL - HALLWAY - NIGHT

Two large Hungarian AGENTS keep watch.

INT. KEMPINSKI HOTEL/EVAN'S SUITE - NIGHT

The lights are low. The fireplace glows. Anna and Evan
sit on the floor before it, sipping wine. Between them,
a coffee table with an ornate chess set.

                    ANNA
          I'm afraid Styles will not be
          back to collect you until morning.

                    EVAN
          What a tragedy.

She leans forward, flashing a lethal dose of cleavage.

                    ANNA
                (re: the room)
          I hope everything is satisfactory?

                    EVAN
          Like staying at the Playboy
          Mansion.

                    ANNA
          You are very quick. Not too
          quick, I hope.

                    EVAN
          Molasses in winter.

                    ANNA
          Hmmm? Confident, clever and witty.
          --If I did not know better I
          should think you work for the
          British government, like your--

                    EVAN
          Not bloody likely.

                    ANNA
          It would have been a mistake for
          you to go on to Vienna.

                    EVAN
          Really?

                    ANNA
               (inching closer)
          You will find it much warmer here.

                    EVAN
          Yes, but won't all that warmth
          spoil what is a rather
          exceptional Tokay?

                    ANNA
          You are familiar with Hungarian wine?

                    EVAN
          Isn't everyone?

                    ANNA
          Some people think them too sweet, yes?

                    EVAN
          Not at all. It pairs perfectly with
          detention, don't you think?

                    ANNA
          You are not so very clever as you
          think. I do not detain. I wish
          only to help.

                    EVAN
          That's a relief.

                    ANNA
          Why do you persist with this defiance?
          There is much at stake here. You have
          no idea what you are up against. Do
          you think this is some kind of game?

                    EVAN
          What makes you think Rhodes'
          life is a game to me?

Reading the determination in his face, she relents, sips
her wine, then moves to within kissing distance.

                    ANNA
          I do apologise. I did not intend
          to sound so callous. It is just
          that we have so little time and
          I am very much interested in
          reaching the climax to this affair.

                         EVAN
        Yes, that would be most gratifying.

She delivers soft, gentle kisses on his lips and face.

                         ANNA
        Perhaps I can be of some assistance?

                         EVAN
        Assistance?

                         ANNA
        Surely you would prefer my company
        for the evening to that of our men
        on the other side of the door, no?

                         EVAN
        Immeasurably.

                         ANNA
        So, how shall we fill the evening?

                         EVAN
                   (re: chessboard)
        Fancy a match?

                         ANNA
        I've a better idea.

She leans in, kisses him, pushing them back onto the floor.

EXT. BUDAPEST STREET - NIGHT

Handkerchief and Handycam watch the hotel from a car.

INT. EVAN'S HOTEL SUITE - MORNING

Evan dresses. Anna carries in tray of food.

                         ANNA
        This should renew your energy. We
        have green figs, yogurt and coffee.

                         EVAN
        No tea?

                         ANNA
        Quickly, Styles is waiting.

                    EVAN
        So soon? Tragic that.

                    ANNA
        Another time, perhaps.

                    EVAN
        I look forward to that.

INT. KAZALI'S CHAMBER - DAY

Kazali and Slatovak video conference with Rhumadi via a
colossal wall-mounted TV.

                    RHUMANDI
        Gentlemen? Are we on schedule?

                    KAZALI
        We are ready now, Excellency.

                    RHUMANDI
        And the weather?

                    KAZALI
        All reports are favourable.

                    RHUMANDI
        How long does the good Dr. Martini
        calculate the northern hemisphere
        to remain uninhabitable?

                    KAZALI
        Combined with our "ground assault",
        that portion of the globe should
        be uninhabitable for approximately
        eighteen to twenty-four months.

                    RHUMANDI
        Excellent! And the Rhodes boy?

                    KAZALI
        That should be remedied any minute now.

Like little boys torturing insects, they share a laugh.

EXT. BUDAPEST STREET - DAY

As Evan and Anna emerge from the hotel, Styles quickly
ushers them into a car.

In a distant, parked car, Handkerchief aims an oozy. As Handycam takes aim from behind the corner of a façade.

INT. CAR - DAY

Large male DRIVER, 35, is at wheel, as Styles, Anna and Evan slide quickly into the car.

>   STYLES
>   (to driver)
>   Let's go--

Suddenly, a hail of gunfire shatters the DRIVER's window and he slumps onto the steering wheel. Anna shoves Evan down as she and Styles try to return fire.

>   ANNA
>   Stay down.

>   EVAN
>   (to self)
>   Not this again!

EXT. BUDAPEST STREET - DAY

Handycam, and Handkerchief, unleash a bullet barrage.

Shocked by what she has seen, a MIDDLE-AGE-WOMAN, groceries in hand, shrieks. Handycam turns upon her. Evan tries for her, but is held back by Anna and can only watch as Handycam guns the woman down.

Outgunned, Styles and Anna toss out their weapons. Handycam runs over, opens the driver door and yanks the DRIVER's body out and into the street.

>   HANDYCAM
>   (to Styles)
>   Drive!

Styles slides behind the wheel. Handycam climbs in next to him. Handkerchief takes the rear, centering Evan.

>   HANDYCAM (cont.)
>   Go! Quickly!

> EVAN
> (to Styles)
> Yes, quickly. Don't you see our
> man here is on a mission? God
> knows how many more middle-aged
> women need dealing with.

Handkerchief quickly throws an elbow into Evan's head.

> HANDKERCHIEF
> Shut it!

> STYLES
> (to Evan)
> Stay calm, sir.

> HANDYCAM
> (to Styles)
> Drive!

Checking Evan's wound, Anna carefully nudges Evan
forward enough to obstruct Handkerchief's view of her
lap, as she slowly, reaches up and under her skirt.

> HANDYCAM (cont.)
> Turn here!

INT. CAR - DAY

The car enters the deserted lane, save for a lone VAN.

> HANDYCAM (cont.)
> Stop!

The car stops short.

> HANDYCAM (cont.)
> Out!

Anna quickly pulls out a pistol from under her skirt.
Then, with the precision of an Old West gunslinger,
sends a bullet into the foreheads of Handycam and
Handkerchief, before either can get off a shot.

> STYLES
> (to Evan)
> All right, sir?

                    EVAN
          Nothing broken, if that's
          what you mean?

Anna re-checks his wound.

                    ANNA
          Good. I'm very glad you weren't
          hurt too badly.

                    EVAN
          You're glad?

                    ANNA
          Now, only one more detail.

                    STYLES
          What's that?

Anna raises her gun and quickly fires into Styles'
forehead, then aims at Evan.

                    ANNA
          Now, very, very carefully, get
          out of the car and into that van.

Evan looks at dead assassins, then at her.

                    ANNA (cont.)
          A bullet to the face is best, it
          helps to vanquish the memory of them.

                    EVAN
          Why kill them if they work for you?

                    ANNE
          Now, I don't have to pay them

                    EVAN
          The ice cold, double agent, blonde.
          How cliché!

                    ANNA
          Out!

EXT. ALLEY - DAY

Aiming at Evan, Anna backs out of the car. With remote,
she opens the van door.

                    ANNA
          Now, be a good boy, and do as
          you're told. It would be a
          shame to end pretty you. --Now
          get out! ...Go to the van. Get
          in! --Carefully!

Evan complies, spots a pair of handcuffs hanging, with
one end attached to inner the frame of the van.

                    ANNA (cont.)
          Lock one hand into the cuff.

                    EVAN
          A little foreplay, then?

                    ANNA
          Regretfully, no. --Quickly!

Evan does as ordered. Anna slides the door closed then
hurries round to the wheel, climbs in and blasts off.

EXT. HUNGARIAN COUNTRYSIDE - DAY

Anna's van speeds through the lush area, before braking
to a hard stop.

INT. VAN - DAY

Evan peers through the window for a clue. Nothing, only
the SOUND of Anna's quick moving steps heading to the
door. It opens. Anna stands, taking aim.

                    ANNA
          Good night, my sweet.

She fires. The force of the shot slams Evan up against
the inner panel, out.

Anna reaches in, removes a winged dart from Evan's side,
then yanks a soldier-like-jumpsuit from a duffel bag,
slips it over her outfit and slams the door.

INT. UNDERGROUND FACILITY - DAY

The long, narrow, dimly-lit room is home to rows of
tables, packed to capacity with petri dishes of growing
cultures, which dozens of bee-like WORKERS in HAZMAT
suits tend to.

As Kazali inspects progress, Dr. Martini follows
nervously. His drooping shoulders reveal a beaten man.

                    KAZALI
          And so, my good doctor, things
          are progressing well, no?

Dr. Martini answers with a nervous nod.

                    KAZALI (cont.)
          And our chances of complete success?

                    DR. MARTINI
          If the weather is cooperative, the
          cloud you send up will infect the
          whole of Europe and Russia. And,
          eventually, North America. Though
          much of the bacteria's strength
          will have dissipated by then.

                    KAZALI
          Do not worry, doctor. We have
          not forgotten about that self-
          inflated country of yours.

                    DR. MARTINI
          And my family?

                    KAZALI
          I have not forgotten them, either.

                    DR. MARTINI
          But we're sending disease into
          their air?

                    KAZALI
          Depending upon the results of
          your work, I shall have them
          moved, or planted into the earth.
          It is in your hands, my friend.

                    DR. MARTINI
          But I've done all that you--

                    KAZALI
          Then have no fear. Where would
          you like them to go? Australia? No,
          too much like America. --New
          Zealand is better, no?

Overwrought, Dr. Martini drops to his knees, takes
Kazali's hand and grovels. Disgusted, Kazali exits.

A SOLDIER, also repelled, forcefully grabs the doctor's
arm, lifts him to his feet and shoves him back to work.

INT. ASSEMBLY ROOM - DAY

Mannington briefs a room full of AGENTS.

> MANNINGTON
> As you are all aware, we've four
> days to the deadline, a threat we
> are taking very seriously. --Time,
> ladies and gentlemen, is running
> out. Therefore, the PM and I have
> decided to triple the number of
> operatives in the field. --I don't
> care how many doors we have to kick
> in, or how many rocks we have to
> turn over. I want these vermin put
> out of business for good! Jammisson
> will supply you with your individual
> assignments. That is all. Good luck!

He marches forthright out of the room.

EXT. FERIHEY AIRPORT/STREET - DAY

Milo, standing by his car, embraces Michelle as she
emerges from the airport terminal.

INT. KAZALI'S CHAMBER - DAY

Kazali, Slatovak and Anna enjoy opera and brandy as
Evan, limp in a chair, slowly regains consciousness.

> KAZALI
> Ah, my dear Professor, you have
> decided to join us. I was
> beginning to think my best man
> (re: Anna)
> here had been too rough with you.

Foggily, Evan surveys the stark, cloud-like chamber as
Anna delivers a brandy and reviving helping of cleavage.

> EVAN
> So this is heaven?

                         KAZALI
          Not quite. But rest assured,
          that is your final destination.

                         EVAN
          Really? I could have sworn I had
          already been on the wrong end of--

                         ANNA
          A tranquilizer, my sweet. I have
          no wish to forget your lovely face.

Kazali and Slatovak chuckle at the comment.

                         KAZALI
          Patience, Professor. You will be
          on your way to that great classroom
          in the sky soon. But first, a surprise.

Kazail reaches over his desk, presses a key on a control
panel. The door opens and TWO SOLDIERS march in.

                         KAZALI (cont.)
          Place him with our esteemed guest.

The soldiers take hold of Evan and shove him out, a
sight that causes the villains to burst into laughter.

EXT. TRAIN STATION - VIENNA - MORNING

Karl and authorities slide open a carriage and rip into
the "Red Cross" crates. The MUSTACHES beam as only
medical supplies are found. Karl snarls.

INT. MANNINGTON'S OFFICE - DAY

Mannington, Jammisson and TWO AGENTS review a map spread
over the desk. The phone interrupts. Jammisson finds the
phone under the map, answers, listens, then rings off.

                         MANNINGTON
          Well?

                         JAMMISSON
          Styles is dead. No sign of the
          Rhodes boy.

Mannington drops into his chair.

INT. UNDERGROUND CORRIDOR - DAY

Two SOLDIERS lead Evan to Rhodes' cell, open the door
and shove him inside.

INT. RHODES' HOLDING CELL - DAY

Rhodes and Evan are stunned by the sight of one another.
Their silence is weighty.

                    RHODES
          Dr. Tydfil, I presume?

Gobsmacked, Evan offers nothing.

                    RHODES (cont.)
          Splendid to meet you. I'm Rhodes.

Again nothing.

                    RHODES (cont.)
                    (re: cell)
          Quite charming, this, actually.
          I've seen worse. ...So, you've met
          Nigel, then?

Confusion paints Evan's face.

                    RHODES (cont.)
          Mannington. Nigel Mannington?

Evan answers with a quick nod.

                    RHODES (cont.)
          Then what on earth are you doing
          here? This is the point of no--

                    EVAN
          I crossed that when I found-- You
          remember my mother, don't you? Oh
          wait, let me guess, spies don't cry?

Pained, Rhodes takes seat on the cot.

                    EVAN (cont.)
          I'm glad to see you're so broken
          up. I'll be sure to mention that
          when I visit her grave.

<pre>
                    RHODES
         Provided you get out of here first.

Evan looks over the cell, his face sinks.

EXT. HUNGARIAN COUNTRYSIDE - DAY

A car treads turtle-like along the road.

INT. CAR - DAY

Jammisson and TWO AGENTS, survey the area.

                    AGENT #1
         The local police who found Styles'
         body, canvased this entire area
         without success--

                    JAMMISSON
         I will not have the boy's body
         lingering in a ditch!

In the distance, a VAN approaches. They pay it no mind.
Suddenly, the van rams into the car. THREE MASKED MEN,
Kevlar vests over fatigues, jump out firing.

AGENTS #1 and #2 attempt to fire, but are hit without
getting off a shot. Jammisson is hit in the chest.

EXT. HUNGARIAN COUNTRYSIDE - DAY

Agents in the car slump over. MASK #1 opens the car
door, yanks out Jammisson's body. He and MASK #2 take it
with them into the van and speed away.

INT. VAN - DAY

Mask #1 rips open Jammisson's shirt, revealing a Kevlar
vest, then taps his face.

                    MASK #1
         All right, sir?

                    JAMMISSON
                    (coming round)
         Absolutely.

Mask #1 pulls off his mask, it's Slatovak.
</pre>

                    SLATOVAK
              Excellent!

EXT. HUNGARIAN COUNTRYSIDE - DAY

The van veers off road, onto a grassy patch where it
stops before a waiting helicopter.

Slatovak and a SOLDIER burst out of the van and assist
Jammisson aboard the aircraft. The driver dumps the van
in the adjacent river, then boards the chopper.

INT. HOLDING CELL - DAY

Rhodes, seated on cot, studies a pacing Evan. Suddenly,
THREE SOLDIERS charge in.

                    SOLDIER #1
              Come.

                    RHODES
                 (to Evan)
              Very impressive economic use of
              the language. Don't you think?

The soldiers push them out.

INT. CORRIDOR - DAY

Soldiers lead father and son through a corridor maze.

INT. KAZALI'S CHAMBER - DAY

Kazali, cigar in hand, and Anna, on settee, feet up,
lounging, gloat as Evan and Rhodes are ushered in.

                    KAZALI
              Ah, gentlemen, do join us. Professor,
              I trust you have introduced yourself
              to my good friend Mr. Rhodes, here?

Nothing.

                    KAZALI (cont.)
              Good lord! Not quite the reunion I
              had intended. In fact, I am rather
              disappointed. For, such family
              dysfunction pains me.

SOLDIERS shove Evan and Rhodes into seats. One delivers gin and tonics all round.

                    KAZALI (cont.)
          Well, professor, tell me. What do
          you think of my subterranean fortress?

                    EVAN
          A little more elaborate burrow,
          perhaps, but a rodent dwelling
          nonetheless.

                    KAZALI
          That's quite a tongue, my boy.
          (looks up at wall-mounted swords)
          Perhaps I shall cut it out.

Anna chuckles, causing her G&T to go down wrongly.

INT. CAR - DAY

Milo at the wheel. Michelle keeps watch.

                    MICHELLE
          How much further--

A helicopter suddenly appears in the sky before them.
The aircraft descends, disappearing into the forest.

                    MICHELLE (cont.)
          Arret! Arret! --Stop!

POV - MICHELLE AND MILO

Through the trees they watch as Jammisson and Slatovak
disembark the aircraft and stride into the old barn.

END POV

                    MILO
          What is this place?

INT. KAZALI'S CHAMBER - DAY

                    KAZALI
               (to Evan and Rhodes)
          Gentleman, your undivided
          attention, if you please.

With pointer in hand, Kazali points out a location on
the huge world map mounted onto the wall.

                    KAZALI (cont.)
        This gentlemen, is where we are,
        500 kilometers to the west of Lodz.
        And here gentlemen, is Warsaw.
        Notice its position. Perfectly
        centered between London and Moscow.

                    RHODES
        Oh, I see, you've purchased a villa
        in Warsaw so you can shop at Harrod's
        in the morning and still attend the
        Bolshoi in the evening?

                    KAZALI
        An excellent suggestion. I must make
        note of that. But for the moment, if
        you would kindly bestow your patience
        upon me, I assure you, you will find
        my presentation most interesting.

                    RHODES
        We're all ears.

                    KAZALI
        Would you care for a cigar?

                    RHODES
        Geography lessons just aren't the
        same without them. Don't you agree?

                    KAZALI
                    (to Anna)
        Would you mind?

He gestures at the cigar box on his desk.

                    ANNA
        Not at all, I am handsomely
        paid to serve.

                    KAZALI
        Ah, yes, money, the great equalizer.

Anna delivers the box to Rhodes.

> RHODES
>
> Why how thoughtful, my dear.

> ANNA
> (to EVAN)
> And for you, my sweet?

Nothing.

> ANNA (cont.)
> Oh, lost the mood, eh?

> EVAN
> On the contrary, I'm aching
> to get my hands on you.

Anna snarls.

> KAZALI
> (to Rhodes)
> Since we have had such a good
> rapport, you and I, over the
> years, I thought I'd share my
> latest little venture with you.
> After all, you have been such
> an inspiration to me.

> RHODES
> I'm overwhelmed.

Kazali returns to the map.

> KAZALI
> You see, my good friend, from
> here, I shall bombard Warsaw
> with bacteria laden missiles.
> This, as you might imagine,
> will produce a cloud of disease
> so massive, its circumference
> will blanket London, Moscow and,
> of course, everything in between.

> RHODES
> Thought of that all by yourself, eh?

> KAZALI
> Do not worry. I have made quite
> certain that, as my very special
> (MORE)

                    KAZALI (cont.)
        guests of honour, you shall have a
        front row seat. His Excellency is
        ever mindful of the great debt he
        owes you. And it shall be repaid.

                    RHODES
        Oh, please. He's not still on about
        that, is he? It was my pleasure.
        I'm only sorry I couldn't have
        helped him with the other ear.

                    KAZALI
        Nevertheless, a debt is a debt. Now,
        if you'll kindly accompany me, I'd
        like to take you on a little tour.

EXT. POLISH COUNTRYSIDE - DUSK

The calm is unnerving calm. The only visible movements
are the swaying trees and Milo and Michelle in the car.

INT. MILO'S CAR - DUSK

                    MILO
        I don't see anything.

                    MICHELLE
        Wait here. I shall take a look.

He takes a very nervous deep breath.

                    MILO
        No. I shall go. I am not afraid.

                    MICHELLE
        Yes you are.

She hands him her mobile phone.

                    MICHELLE (cont.)
        If I am not back in fifteen
        minutes, ring Mannington.

She slips quietly out, and into the trees.

INT. UNDERGROUND FACILITY - DUSK

Kazali stops before a large window.

                    KAZALI
        This, gentlemen, is where I
        incubate my pestilent friends.

POV - EVAN, RHODES AND KAZALI

A chamber full of tables, with petri dishes atop and
HAZMATS tending them.

END POV

                    KAZALI (cont.)
        TES is now the real super power!

                    RHODES
        Yes, but Anthrax?

                    KAZALI
        True, it is a crude, peasant
        weapon, yes. But it is inexpensive
        and very, very easy to produce.
        And did I mention, very effective?

                    RHODES
        Rule the world. In a different
        key, perhaps, but still the same
        old, worn out, tune, I'm afraid.

                    KAZALI
        My dear Mr. Rhodes, what we are
        undertaking here is a new beginning.
        Save for a small percentage of humankind,
        people are a vile, worthless lot. They
        will never achieve peace in the world,
        nor anything truly wondrous, save for
        opera, of course.

                    RHODES
                    (to Evan)
        He obviously hasn't discovered
        crème brulee.

                    EVAN
        Obviously.

                    KAZALI
        Come now, the species has had
        centuries to realise its humanity.
                    (MORE)

                    KAZALI (cont.)
Yet it has failed. Its infancy must
end. It is time for it to move into
adolescence. With one exception--

                    RHODES
But of course.

                    KAZALI
We shall govern. --This way, please.

INT. UNDERGROUND CHAMBER - NIGHT

Kazali and SOLDIERS, lead Rhodes and Evan to a massive
chamber in which dozens of HAZMAT WORKERS assemble a sea
of warheads.

                    KAZALI
Several strategic strikes from our
insulated facility here and we shall
set in motion our solution to the
'people problem' without destroying
a single city. Thus, sparing the
planet from further abuse from its
most ungrateful of inhabitants.

                    EVAN
A tree hugging terrorist? I don't--

                    KAZALI
Why move out of the house simply
because of a few mice?

                    RHODES
Exactly! We can't let a little
thing like genocide ruin a night
at the opera, can we?

Kazali is about to bark back when a SOLDIER escorts a
very distraught Dr. Martini through the corridor.

                    KAZALI
Ah, Dr. Martini. Have you met my
other guests? This is Mr. Rhodes
and his son.

                    RHODES
How do you do, doctor? We must meet
for a drink a little later.

Noticeably trembling, Dr. Martini is unable to speak.

                    KAZALI
        The good doctor has been kind
        enough to assist us in our efforts.

                    RHODES
        How very philanthropic.

Kazali barks in Polish, Martini's led away.

                    RHODES (cont.)
        Nice to have met you, doctor.
                (to Kazali)
        My dear Captain, it's an admirable
        plan. But, I'm afraid anthrax
        simply won't do.

                    KAZALI
        And why is that?

                    RHODES
        Firstly, there's the heat from
        the warhead. Secondly, ultraviolet
        light will destroy much of the
        bacteria once it's exposed to daylight.
        And lastly, there are antibiotics.

                    KAZALI
        Come now, we both know there is simply
        not enough antibiotic to treat the
        infected on a mass scale. Yet, more
        importantly, the very clever doctor has
        developed a more potent and incredibly
        resilient strain by simply adding
        trypsin to the growth culture.

                    EVAN
        The enzyme?

                    KAZALI
        Very good, professor. The good
        doctor estimates his strain to
        be some 400 times stronger. But
        that is not all. ...You see, like
        any good boxer, one does not
        count solely on the a good right
        hand. One must also employ the
        dependable jab, no?

He points to a distant section of the assembly line
where smaller vials of bacteria are being prepared.

                    KAZALI (cont.)
          There, gentlemen, is my jab, botulism.
          --With my super anthrax strain, I must
          release 140 pounds of bacteria just to
          kill a mere three million. To kill 500
          million, a billion, I jab with this.
                    (re: vials)
          It, I shall deposit into the Vistula
          and Odra rivers, subsequently infecting
          the whole of Europe. But please, gentlemen,
          do not fret. This war my comrades and I
          wage upon mankind is intended as merely
          a good cleansing. Nothing more. I assure
          you, it is not the end of the species,
          but simply its glorious rebirth.

                    RHODES
          Amen, brother!

                    KAZALI
          Gentlemen! I speak to you of war
          against the weak within the species--
                    (stops, turns, punches fist in hand)
          ...I speak of an advancement in our
          evolution. Thus, I submit, war is good.

                    EVAN
          You do realise there's no such
          thing as happily ever after.

                    KAZALI
          What you speak of is a different kind
          of happiness. You speak of love, that
          vile, fleeting creature. It is not
          the answer. ...War, sweet war, my
          friends, is everlasting, dependable,
          and, I might add, always very profitable.

                    EVAN
          Strawberries and cream, eh?

                    KAZALI
                    (hands Rhodes a cigar)
          But now, if you will excuse me, I've
          many details to tend to, including
                    (MORE)

                    KAZALI (cont.)
        your itineraries. I promise it to
        be a grand spectacle!

Soldiers usher the father and son away.

EXT. COUNTRYSIDE - NIGHT

Michelle creeps up to the barn. Reaching it, she peers
through the cracks in the boards. Nothing. She slips in.

INT. OLD BARN - NIGHT

Michelle explores the barn, looking for clues in the
straw, unaware of the camouflaged camera above her.

INT. SECURITY CHAMBER - NIGHT

The stark room is filled with video monitors displaying
Michelle's every move. SOLDIERS watch intently. One
SOLDIER, in a Slavic tongue, orders the others off.

INT. OLD BARN - NIGHT

As Michelle quietly examines the barn, several SOLDIERS
spring swiftly upon her. She attempts to scream out, but
her mouth is quickly taped. Hands cuffed behind her, she
is led to the lift.

INT/EXT. MILO'S CAR - NIGHT

Milo nervously studies the dark landscape for a sign of
Michelle. Nothing! He checks his watch, then grabs
Michelle's phone, when out of nowhere, SOLDIERS converge
upon him, yank him out of the car, tape his mouth and
handcuff him.

INT. RHODES' HOLDING CELL - NIGHT

Evan surveys the corridor through the door window.
Rhodes seated on the cot, lights up his cigar.

                    RHODES
        We're very fortunate, you and I.
        We might have been taken captive
        by a more common, unsophisticated
        psychopath. The kind of psychopath
        who has no appreciation for a
        quality cigar.

                    EVAN
          So, you took Rhumandi's ear.

                    RHODES
          A bit of bad luck, I'm afraid.

                    EVAN
          Rather nice touch, I thought.

                    RHODES
          I was aiming for an eye.

                    EVAN
          What? The great spy missed?

                    RHODES
          Well, what can I say? Either the
          sea got rougher, or there were
          one too many pink gins about.

Again, through the cell door window, Evan checks the
corridor. It's clear. He then raises his sleeve to
reveal Milo's watch and takes aim at the door's keyhole.

                    RHODES (cont.)
          Where the hell did you--

                    EVAN
          A friend of a friend.

                    RHODES
          I spent 35 years in the field to
          keep you away from the likes of
          such people.

                    EVAN
          Those people are your bleedin'
          admirers.

He's a touch clumsy trying to operate the watch's laser.

                    RHODES
          My friends would have had the
          decency to show you how to work
          the bloody thing-- Here, give it--

                    EVAN
          I've got it.

The beam shoots out, very nearly hitting Rhodes' hand.

                    EVAN (cont.)
          Apologies! Not quite used to all
          this James Bond madness, yet.

As Evan fires beam into the keyhole, Rhodes is lookout.

                    RHODES
          I would have gladly gone to my
          death to keep you from such
          things. And now look--

                    EVAN
          Oh, don't be so bloody melodramatic.

                    RHODES
          Don't be so bloody ungrateful.

                    EVAN
          Ungrateful? I spent my whole life
          treasuring the memory of a man who
          wasn't even my father. Any idea
          how that makes me feel?

                    RHODES
          You think I wanted that?

                    EVAN
          Spy or no spy, I would have never--

                    RHODES
          What? --You were saying?

Evan fumbles with the laser.

                    RHODES (cont.)
          My life has been about sacrifice.
          I'm not happy about it. Never
          have been-- Sometimes we're
          forced to-- Don't think for
          one moment that I don't feel,
          that I don't-- Here, give me that.

Rhodes takes laser watch from Evan.

                    RHODES (cont.)
          Wow, this model is a real antique.

Rhodes fires the laser into lock. POW! The lock gives.

>   EVAN
>   It worked! It really worked!

>   RHODES
>   We may be a bit past it, we older
>   models, but we still have some
>   fight left in us.

They cautiously slip through the door.

INT. INTERROGATION CHAMBER - NIGHT

The chamber is bare, save for a simple metal table and
chairs. Anna, with 45mm stuck in her belt, hovers over
Michelle, who is handcuffed to a chair.

>   ANNA
>   So, you are Evan's little friend?
>   How lovely. He's very attractive,
>   no? You are in love with him, yes?
>   But of course, you are. Why else
>   do you take this foolish risk?
>   (tauntingly close)
>   I, too, am quite fond of him.
>   The smell of his hair, his skin--

Michelle leans forward, spiting into Anna's face.

>   ANNA
>   You bitch!

Anna delivers a fierce backhand to Michelle's cheek.

EXT. CORRIDOR INTERSECTION - NIGHT

>   EVAN
>   If MI6 had gone after you, they'd--

>   RHODES
>   The device is the priority.

>   EVAN
>   But we're in the bloody device.

>   RHODES
>   It's procedure.

                        EVAN
          Would it be against procedure to
          ask how you and mum really met?

                        RHODES
          At the symphony de Monte Carlo.

                        EVAN
          And?

                        RHODES
          She was stunning, so well read,
          but it was her humanity that
          touched me most. I saw the dark
          side of the world, she saw its
          potential-- Shhh!

Rhodes and Evan quickly step back.

As TWO SOLDIERS pass, father and son jump them. Evan
punches his man into oblivion. Rhodes takes his man from
behind, grabs the soldier's belt-knife and stabs him.

                        EVAN
          What the-- Why?

                        RHODES
          Because I had to.

                        EVAN
          I thought all this is about
          saving lives?

                        RHODES
          You think they wouldn't have
          killed us?

                        EVAN
          But, my God, you did it so easily.
          Have you forgotten your Socrates,
          Aristotle--

                        RHODES
          This isn't the classroom. The
          only philosophers these bastards
          understand are Smith and Wesson--
                    (he spots a narrow door)
          ...In there, quickly!

Evan is frozen.

>   RHODES (cont.)
>   Look, it's never easy. But if there
>   was another way to deal with these
>   bloodthirsty testosterone cases,
>   believe me, I'd welcome it.

Regretfully, Evan snaps to it and drags his man off.
Rhodes struggles with his. Evan pitches in.

>   RHODES (cont.)
>   I'm much too old for this.

INT. GENERATOR CHAMBER - NIGHT

The clamour of a room of electrical generators is harsh.

>   RHODES
>   Get into his clothes. --Quickly!

INT. INTERROGATION CHAMBER - NIGHT

Pacing the room, Anna fights back a swelling anger.

>   ANNA
>   I think I shall chain Evan's arms
>   and legs, while you watch, helplessly,
>   as have my way with him. After which,
>   I shall put a bullet in both of you.

Suddenly, a SOLDIER bursts in, heaving Milo inside.

>   ANNA (cont.)
>   Ah, I see you have brought a friend.
>   (to Milo)
>   My dear, Milo. It would appear you
>   are simply determined to make the
>   little woman the widow, yes?

Milo faints into the soldier's arms.

>   ANNA
>   (to Soldier)
>   Leave him to me and go!

He lets Milo drop, then marches out.

INT. CORRIDOR - NIGHT

In uniform, Evan and Rhodes, move cautiously. Passing an
open door, they spot workers getting into HAZMATs suits
and slip into the room.

INT. DRESSING CHAMBER - NIGHT

Rhodes and Evan do like the others, then follow them
through yet another wide door.

INT. WARHEAD ASSEMBLY CHAMBER - NIGHT

In HAZMAT suits, Evan and Rhodes blend in with the
assembly of workers in the enormous chamber. Some wheel
trollies with petri dishes. Others load warheads.

As Evan and Rhodes survey the activity, a SUPERVISOR
waves them to nearby trollies. They each grab one. TWO
HAZMAT SUITS enter the room and are saluted. They glance
over the progress, then leave.

Pushing trollies, Rhodes and Evan follow. Through the
door window, they watch the two men remove their suits.
It is Jammisson alongside Kazali.

                    RHODES
          I'm going to need a plastic
          bag of my own.

As villains leave, father and son abandon trollies,
enter the room, quickly remove their suits and follow.

INT. CORRIDOR - NIGHT

Evan and Rhodes follow Kazali and Jammisson. Kazali's
senses something behind him. But before he can turn
round, father and son quickly dash through an unmarked door.

INT. INTERROGATION CHAMBER - NIGHT

To everyone's surprise, Evan and Rhodes have stumbled
into Anna's interrogation. She immediately takes aim.

                    EVAN
          Please pardon the intrusion.

                    ANNA
        Not at all. Actually, we were
        just speaking of you.

                    EVAN
        Nothing bad, I hope.

He inches his way towards her.

                    ANNA
        One could never speak badly of you.

Evan scans the room. She aims from the hip.

                    EVAN
        What, no Tokay? It's so unlike
        you to interrogate without it.

                    ANNA
        I'll have some brought in, shall I?

                    EVAN
        Awfully considerate, but we're a
        little short on time.

Inching closer, Evan checks his watch.

                    ANNA
        That is an understatement.

Suddenly the laser beam streams from the watch, striking
her gun hand. Then, just as quickly, Evan sends her to
the floor, and out, with a heavy right hand.

                    EVAN
                (to Michelle/Milo)
        What the hell are you doing here?

Evan kicks Anna's gun over to Rhodes, whilst Milo
locates a key in Anna's pocket and hands it to Evan.

                    EVAN (cont.)
        Come on, let's get out of here.

He un-cuffs Michelle. She throws her arms around his
neck, hugs tightly, then pulls back and slaps him hard.

                    MICHELLE
        You touched her!

Like a boxing referee, Milo quickly stands between them.

                    MILO
          He could never! She is evil!

                    EVAN
               (to Michelle)
          I'd sooner kiss Kazali.

                    RHODES
          I hate to interrupt, but--

                    EVAN
               (to Michelle/Milo)
          This is Rho-- Ah, my father.

Evan and Rhodes briefly lock eyes.

                    MICHELLE
          We once met--

                    RHODES
          Paris. Yes. I never forget a
          beautiful face. Lovely to see
          you again. --Now, what say we
          get the bloody hell out of here?

Rhodes opens the door and all charge out.

INT. CORRIDOR - NIGHT

Rhodes, Evan, Michelle and Milo creep along.

                    EVAN
          Now what?

                    RHODES
          There's never a cow around to kick
          over a lantern when you need one.

                    EVAN
          A fire?

                    RHODES
          Nothing like a good fire to rid
          a place of the plague. --Come on.

They hurry on.

INT. ANOTHER CORRIDOR - NIGHT

The group peeks through a door window.

POV THE GROUP'S

Inside is a vast room, home to rocket launchers and dozens of missiles. Whilst most HAZMAT WORKERS install warheads onto missiles, a FEW are armed and supervising.

In a far corner a stockpile of crates stamped EXPLOZIV. Rhodes notices adjoining decontamination room filled with HAZMAT suits, as well as firearms, is empty.

The group slips inside.

INT. DECONTAMINATION CHAMBER - NIGHT

Evan, Rhodes, Michelle and Milo enter and jump into suits. Rhodes grabs two semi-automatic rifles, tossing one to Evan.

>   RHODES
>   Look, there is no other way--

Evan takes a deep, preparatory breath.

>   RHODES (cont.)
>   All right?

Evan nods unconvincingly.

>   RHODES (cont.)
>   Aim for the crates, wait for my
>   signal then just pull. I'll
>   handle the others.

He charges through the doors. Evan follows.

INT. MISSILE CHAMBER - NIGHT

Rhodes, Evan burst in. Rhodes quickly picks off his men.

>   RHODES
>   Now!

Evan fires upon the crates, unleashing mayhem and panic. A wounded SOLDIER aims for Rhodes, Evan quickly shoots him. Again, he and Rhodes lock eyes before blasting out.

INT. DECONTAMINATION CHAMBER - NIGHT

Father and son charge into the chamber. Rhodes jams a
rifle through the door handles, tossing one to Michelle.

Evan mourns his deed.

> RHODES
> Don't worry. You can't lose
> your soul over these vermin.
> (to all)
> Let's move!

With surprise, Evan spots the weapon in Michelle's hand.

> MICHELLE
> You hear him, let's go!

INT. CORRIDOR - NIGHT

A siren blares away. SOLDIERS rush to the scene. Rhodes
and group quickly dash into another corridor.

They reach the lab, in which panicked workers flee. Evan
spots Dr. Martini in the pack and pulls him aside.

> EVAN
> This way, doctor.

INT. KAZALI'S CHAMBER - NIGHT

Kazali barks into the phone, while Jammisson peeks at
video monitors showing every inch of the facility.

> KAZALI
> (into phone)
> Instruct personnel evacuate the
> facility without panic-- Now!

ON SCREEN, Rhodes' empty holding cell.

Kazali screams out, hurls the phone across the room,
yanks the swords off the wall, tossing one to Jammisson.

> KAZALI
> I will have their heads!

He storms out.

INT. CORRIDOR - NIGHT

Viktor, Slatovak, ready with squadron of soldiers.
Kazali and Jammisson burst in.

> KAZALI
> They are mine! Understand? Mine!

He leads the charge out.

INT. CORRIDOR - NIGHT

Explosions and fires occur everywhere. Panicked
personnel make for the exit. It's a mass of confusion.
Amidst the exodus, Rhodes and group charge through.

> DR. MARTINI
> What are you doing?

> RHODES
> Setting a torch to this God
> forsaken breeding ground.

> DR. MARTINI
> You've done his work for him!

> EVAN
> What? What do you mean, doctor?

> DR. MARTINI
> This facility is completely
> self-contained. You will not be
> able to generate the heat required
> to destroy the cultures. When the
> air runs out, so will the fires.

Evan looks to Rhodes. He thinks, then back to Martini.

> RHODES
> What's the probability of a
> military air strike finishing
> the job?

> DR. MARTINI
> They'll never get here in time
> to stop the spread of bacteria.

> RHODES
> We'll bloody see about that.

Gunfire breaks out. Dr. Martini is hit. Evan pulls him along, as the group dives into another corridor.

Rhodes and Michelle return fire. Kazali and men position themselves behind the rubble and the mêlée wages on.

Evan is stunned as Michelle skillfully guns down Viktor.

                    MICHELLE
                    (to Evan)
        What?

INT. INTERROGATION CHAMBER - NIGHT

Anna gets to her feet and wobbles out.

INT. ANOTHER CORRIDOR - NIGHT

Anna appropriates passing SOLDIERS and leads them off.

INT. CORRIDOR - NIGHT

Crossfire is intense. As Rhodes, Evan and Michelle do their best to hold off troops, Milo tends to the doctor.

                    EVAN
        We must get out of here.

                    MICHELLE
        This corridor is too long and
        straight. And there is no cover.
        We cannot make it.

                    RHODES
        Go on, all of you. I'll hold them--

                    EVAN
        We're not leaving without you.

                    RHODES
        I'm not asking. --Now go!

                    EVAN
        I'm not that little boy you had
        to leave behind. We're not leaving!

                    RHODES
        There are the others to think of!

Behind them, 20 yards in the distance, Anna and soldiers arrive and take aim.

> EVAN
> I'll stay. You go with them.

> RHODES
> Don't fight me on this!

> EVAN
> Don't fight me!

Milo spots the trouble, taps Evan's shoulder. All turn to discover the predicament, and drop their weapons.

> ANNA
> You are forcing me to have to put a bullet in that handsome face of yours. Something I would surely hate.

> EVAN
> You'd hate it?

Kazali's men move in and seize weapons. Kazali steps up to Rhodes and drops him with the back of his sword hand. Evan starts for Kazali, but is held back.

> KAZALI
> Mannington's fearless warrior. You have exhausted my patience!

Jammisson smiles as he slowly steps onto Rhodes' hand.

> JAMMISSON
> The pride of MI6. What a joke. It should have been me, not you! I was Mannington's right hand, not you! It was me! But no! Because of you, my entire career has been a complete and utter waste.
> (kicks Rhodes hard)
> While you basked in the glory that should have rightfully been mine, I have been nothing more than a glorified office boy. I helped to train you! Isn't that a laugh?

                    RHODES
Try strawberries.

                    JAMMISSON
What?

                    RHODES
I fear all those sour grapes are
beginning to affect your mood.

Jammisson kicks him, and again Evan is restrained.

                    JAMMISSON
Your insatiable hunger for the
limelight has robbed me of my
glory-- My glory!

                    RHODES
There's nothing glorious about
battling maniacs like Kazali.

                    KAZALI
And we have tangled for the very
last time, my friend. However,
before I take my delight in
killing you, you shall first
have the pleasure of watching me
take your beloved son's head.

                    RHODES
For God's sake! After thirty years
of this rot, haven't you had enough?

                    KAZALI
You may fancy the idea of retiring
on a simple policeman's pension.
But this, this is my passion. It
breathes life into me.

He gestures to Jammisson, who tosses his sword to Evan.

                    KAZALI (cont.)
Now, Mr. Tydfil--

                    EVAN
Rhodes! The name's Evan Rhodes.

                    KAZALI
Well, Mr. Rhodes, I understand
you're quite skilled with a foil.
But let us see what you can do
with a real man's sword, eh?

A battle ensues. Kazali is immediately applies pressure.

                    KAZALI (cont.)
And you call yourself a swordsman?

                    EVAN
You, sir, are nothing more than a
school-yard bully masquerading as
some sort of a Moriarty figure.

                    KAZALI
You wield that Shakespeare-like tongue
much better than you do that sword.

Kazali nicks and sucker punches Evan, as they battle.

                    SLATOVAK
Capitan, we must evacuate!

                    KAZALI
Yes, yes. One moment!

He lunges and the two lock swords with his blade inching
scarily toward Evan's throat.

Suddenly Kazali groans with a painful agony. His face
contorts. He looks at Evan to discover Michelle's pen in
Evan's free hand and plunged into his side.

                    EVAN
                 (to Kazali)
It was never any contest.

Kazali contorts, twists and falls to the floor, dead.

                    RHODES
                 (to Jammisson)
Once again, the mighty pen, eh?

Soldiers start for Evan, but an explosion rocks the
area. As debris cuts Slatovak and soldiers off, Michelle
springs upon Anna for possession of her handgun.

In the mayhem, Jammisson grabs Kazali's sword and starts
for Rhodes, but Evan quickly throws his sword into him.
Shocked, Jammisson, glares at Rhodes, then drops.

Anna, who is getting the better of the clash, flings
Michelle against the wall and takes aim.

Suddenly, a shot rings out, thrusting Anna against the
wall and onto the floor, a bullet hole in her forehead.

                    MILO
                (gun in hand)
        I'm sorry, but I had to!

                    EVAN
        Believe me, she wouldn't have
        wanted it any other way.

As Michelle hugs Milo, Rhodes eyes Jammisson's body.

                    RHODES
        I wanted to fit him with a
        plastic bag of my own.

                    EVAN
        It wouldn't have brought her back.

                    RHODES
        I really loved her! --This
        damned, bloody business-- Losing
        her was the worst day of my life.

                    EVAN
        I know.

Evan rips the phone off Kazali's belt and tosses it over
to Michelle.

                    EVAN (cont.)
        Quickly, cheri. Tell them to send
        the bloody kitchen sink-- Vite!

She dials, as Evan helps, a battered Rhodes to his feet.

                    RHODES
        I'm getting far too old for this.

                    EVAN
        That's not age you feel. Saving the
        world is thirsty business. And I'd
        say you deserve a rather large one,
        on me. --Now, what say we blast out
        of this rat hole?

The group then races through the mayhem.

EXT. POLISH COUNTRYSIDE - DAWN

With volcanic force, explosions rip the area. The group
and scores of workers pour out of the barn.

Martini spots SOLDIERS boarding helicopter.

                    DR. MARTINI
        They're off to infect the rivers!

Evan sprints for it, tackling the LAST of FOUR SOLDIERS.
SOLDIER #2 takes aim.

Michelle quickly picks him off.

As the chopper lifts, Evan overpowers his man then hangs
on to the chopper's landing skid, where he's met by
SOLDIER #3's boot. He quickly grabs the soldier's
trouser leg and yanks him out by it.

INT. HELICOPTER - DAY

Keeping one hand on the stick, SOLDIER #4, piloting the
craft, tries for his sidearm. Evan is quickly on him.

They struggle, the craft rapidly descends. Solider #4
tries to manage both, but Evan delivers a booming right,
slumping his man over the controls.

With a quick look through the windscreen he spots trees
below, then swiftly dives off the craft.

EXT. POLISH COUNTRYSIDE - DAY

As the chopper crashes and explodes in the distance,
Evan's landing, through the trees, is bruising. Stopped
on a low branch, Evan drops to the ground.

Rhodes and Michelle rush to him.

                    RHODES
         They weren't teaching that in
         any of my philosophy courses--
         Can you stand?

Evan nods. The pair help Evan up to his feet and hurry
him to Milo's car.

                    EVAN
         Am I glad to see that old thing!

All hurry into the car. Yet, Milo's erratic attempt to
speed away is thwarted by the thunderous bombardment
upon the facility by the arrival of allied aircraft,
which runs them off the road.

INT. CAR - DAWN

The group crouches down for cover as a wave of debris
and smoke completely engulfs them.

EXT. CEMETARY/WELSH COUNTRYSIDE - DAY

SUPER ON SCREEN: "TWO MONTHS LATER"

Several AGENTS wait by several cars, as Michelle and
Mannington join Rhodes, Evan at Nelly's grave. All stand
silent as Evan and Rhodes place flowers on the grave.

                    RHODES
                 (to grave)
         In the hereafter, my sweet.

Evan throws an arm around Rhodes.

                    MANNINGTON
         That's quite a lad you've got.

                    RHODES
         I know.

                    MANNINGTON
         I apologise for the six weeks of
         quarantine, but we had to take
         every precaution. Especially with
         Michelle in her condition.

EVAN
I understand. I plan to spend a
lifetime watching over her, myself.

He places a hand on her stomach.

MICHELLE
(to Mannington)
You may lock me up with Evan
anytime.
(to Rhodes)
We both enjoyed it, no? It gave
us the time with him, yes?

In the distance a dark car creeps toward them. Also,
behind distant headstones, MUSTACHES take aim. Suddenly,
from the car window, Slatovak fires upon the group.

Evan quickly takes Michelle to the ground. Mannington
and Rhodes also hit the ground.

AGENTS return fire. The car speeds off, but not before
shooters manage to wound Mannington, who drops his gun.

Using headstones as cover, the Mustaches move in. Rhodes
and AGENTS return fire. Two agents are hit.

With bullets flying past, Evan picks up Mannington's
gun. Then, with soldier-like precision, quickly rolls on
the ground and comes up firing, killing both Mustaches.

Calm is restored.

RHODES
I'm much too old for this.

EVAN
(to agents)
Get an ambulance!

MANNINGTON
With your father retired, I could
really use someone with your--

RHODES
No!

Mannington looks to Michelle, then Rhodes, then to Evan.

                    MANNINGTON
      They'll never stop coming.

Stunned, Evan steps back.

                    EVAN
      Let them!

                    MICHELLE
                    (to Rhodes)
      They will not stop, will they?

Rhodes' face of resignation confirms.

                    MANNINGTON
                    (to Evan)
      They'll never stop.

                    EVAN
      I don't care!

Michelle pauses, tears stream down her face.

                    MICHELLE
      My god, my love, I am so happy
      in love with you, but it is now
      just like your parents, n'est-ce
      pas? We have a child of our own
      to think of. We too must make
      the horrible choice--

                    EVAN
      No, we can do this. We worked
      brilliantly together. Didn't we?

Michelle hugs Evan tightly.

                    MICHELLE
      Yes, my luv, yes! ...I love you,
      but as I told you, I know these
      people. They are not simply
      despicable, they are evil, and
      they enjoy it.

                    EVAN
      No!

> MICHELLE
> It will not be easy, I know. But
> we must be strong, and wait, wait
> until we can be together. --Yes,
> I think it is best.

Michelle pulls back, turns to an AGENT.

> MICHELLE (cont.)
> Can you drive me?

The AGENT looks to Mannington, who gives him the nod.

> EVAN
> Wait! Just like that? A decision
> in an instant? …I'm not a spy! I
> am not a spy, for Christ sakes!
> I'm a university professor!

Fighting tears, Michelle gently kisses Evan, then turns,
struggles to collect herself, before she and AGENT walk
toward the parked cars.

Evan looks to Rhodes, then to Mannington, then,
agonizingly, watches Michelle slip out of his life.

> EVAN
> (to himself)
> So, it's true, then. There is no
> such thing as happily ever after.

THE END

www.ingramcontent.com/pod-product-compliance
Lightning Source LLC
Chambersburg PA
CBHW060944040426
42445CB00011B/998